"In this collection of poems about temporary jobs, weak bosses, poor pay, and false choices, Jason Baldinger shows himself as a skilled poet of collapsible dreams. He is the ghost brother of David Lerner, another poet of bad luck litanies and fall down finesse. Baldinger offers his Pittsburgh heart, his verbal artistry, and his expansive presence. He offers characters who stubbornly keep driving even when there is no road ahead."

-Mike James, author of *Jumping Drawbridges in Technicolor*

"Jason Baldinger's poetry is an artifact of a life richly lived with a keen awareness of the intersection of history, individual dreams, and an American realism of a country finally willing to assess itself seriously. Baldinger's America is one built on the backs of the labor of others, one where the payments only cover the interest and never touch the principal, and one where the class struggles of our grandparents are eternally present if you know where to look. The book you are holding in your hands is a new vision of Kerouac's dream of the recording angel."

-Matt Ussia, author of *The Red Glass Cat*

"In *A History of Backroads Misplaced* Jason Baldinger demonstrates his limitless wonder and unyielding weariness with our world almost immediately and the further you travel with him through these selected poems, the more you see how he intricately crosshatches the valleyed expanse between rugged and tender, how he reveals the vulnerable crick in his neck, how he fans out every shade of grey like a riverboat gambler throwing down a full house to the dismay of the rubes sitting at the table with him. "

-Steve Brightman, author of *The Circus of his Bones*

"In this gritty, neo-beat-spiritual collection, the poet is searching and scavenging for answers—is heaven really on the other side of the bar, is God's image found in the toilet water vomit reflection, how many hymns does it take? Whatever the answer, listen to the big voice (that resembles your mother's) behind these poems: go home, clean yourself up, and saunter along again under the big blue sky tomorrow."

-Linzi Garcia, author of *Thank You*

"In a history of backroads misplaced Jason Baldinger takes us on journeys along the backroads and highways of America, as well as deep within his hometown of Pittsburgh. Spending time in neighborhood bars, diners, and shit jobs, Baldinger doesn't just pass through a place, he inhabits it in a way few travelers do with language both precise and relaxed. It is a gift he shares with us in this generous volume."

-M. J. Arcangelini, author of *A Quiet Ghost*

a history of backroads misplaced
(selected poems 2010-2020)

Jason Baldinger

Kung Fu Treachery Press
Rancho Cucamonga, CA

Copyright © Jason Baldinger, 2021
First Edition: 1 3 5 7 9 10 8 6 4 2
ISBN: 978-1-952411-80-9
LCCN: 2021949591

Cover image: Jon Dowling
Author photos: Alanna Miles
All rights reserved. No part of this publication may be reproduced or transmitted in any form or by any means, electronic or mechanical, including photocopying, recording or by info retrieval system, without prior written permission from the author.

Acknowledgments

It's been a decade since I put out my first book in 2010 on Six Gallery Press, a book I split with Jerome Crooks called the *Whiskey Rebellion*. In that time I can't tally all the bars, small towns, diners and cafés, motels, couches and highways I've traced, crashed, ate or died in. There are a lot of people to thank over that time and I'm sure I'll forget more than my fair share, (and if I forgot you, you are appreciated and I'm sorry). So thanks to Scott Silsbe, Bob Pajich, Mark Mangini, Kris Collins, Nathan Kukulski, Jon Dowling, Rob Gray, Dianne Borsenik, Matt Borczon, Jay Miner, Matt Ussia, Don Wentworth, Jason Ryberg, James Benger, John Dorsey, Victor Clevenger, Stephanie Brea, Alanna Miles, Karl Hendricks, Jeanette Powers, Nell Hendricks, Josh Delisle, Joe Archangelini, Steve Brightman, John Burroughs, Chandra Adelman, Linzi Garcia, Mike James, Jerome Crooks, Nikki Allen, Renee Alberts, Mark McLane and Osage County Arts Community, Shawn Pavey, Mark Bruseke, Alan Butera, Kat Giordano, Dan Wright, John Patrick Robbins, Red Bob, Lori Jakiela, Dave Newman, Jimmy Cvetic, Joan Bauer, Jen Quinio, Jesse Quinn Alperin and Steve Pellegrino

Some poems here previously appeared in *The Dope Fiend Daily, Outlaw Poetry, Uppagus, Lilliput Review, Rusty Truck, Dirtbag Review, Red Eft Review, In Between Hangovers, Your One Phone Call, Winedrunk Sidewalk, Anti-Heroin Chic, Nerve Cowboy Concrete Meat Press, Zombie Logic Press, Ramingo's Porch, Rye Whiskey Review, Red Fez, Mad Swirl, Blue Hour Review, Mojave River Review, Cajun Mutt Press, Duane's PoeTree, Chiron Review, Fixator Press, Vox Populi, As It Ought To Be, Black Coffee Review, North of Oxford, Chiron Review, Heartland! Poetry of Love, Solidarity and Resistance, Heroin Love Songs, Rust Belt Press Review, River Dog, Rust Belt Press, The Gasconade Review.*

destination schedule:

introduction by victor clevenger

utopia / 1
new straitsville / 3
windber / 5
life with lions / 8
holy ghost / 10
dead man's hymn / 12
berkman / 13
sarah anne / 18
betty / 20
ray / 24
the hymn to toilet duck / 26
my three days as an environmentalist / 29
hymn at the end / 32
the ballad of mickey mantle / 34
hymn to free's *fire and water* / 37
I came up empty / 40
the old weird america / 41
I am rain / 42
the ballad of forty mosquitos / 45
these days of heaven / 47
back when we were wild / 50
the museum club / 51
goodbye pacific ocean blue / 53
zen and the western sunset / 55
hymn to the immaculate heart of mary / 57
hymn to inevitability / 59
sam / 62

hymn to grease / 65

winter of office supplies / 68

heaven / 71

he said only eat half / 73

a rabbit from hell / 76

the man who sees underground / 78

half day hymn / 81

last call / 83

only love can break your heart / 86

the bird songs tonight / 88

hold on cool breeze / 90

take a break / 92

some summers drop like files / 93

tell me why / 94

better luck next year / 96

here's to your ex-wife / 98

fuck you jay gatsby / 100

the ballad of dylan and jake / 102

it was a town called yukon / 104

hagerstown sometimes / 106

redneck's paradise / 107

like neil young in *albuquerque* / 108

the great american apple pie fight / 110

tony brush park has sinks and restrooms / 111

pavey at the waffle house / 116

al's bar / 117

dial s for sonny / 118

riggs lounge / 128

between cedarville and pearl / 129

109 n. graham / 130

9 stories / 131
beechwood farms / 132
evening watch / 133
mescaline / 134
reasons to hate being poor / 135
susquehanna river blues / 136
fric and frac / 137
39th street blues / 138
union hill prayer / 139
mizzou / 140
indiana billboard (found poem) / 141
new year's day / 142
for the beloved dead of delaware / 143
cielito lindo / 145
for anna karina / 147
winner winner chicken dinner / 148
unconditional surrender / 150
payphone hymnals / 153
4113 bethoven / 155
jumbotron / 156
solaris / 158
we own the night / 160
zoloft / 163
icon / 166
postcard from belle missouri / 168
the glory hole / 170
oscar's diner / 171
winter 1979 / 172
wilmerding / 175
the blue haven / 176

hymn to garfield hill / 178
the great pittsburgh pierogie race a'nat / 179
the night the fireflies taught
   dave brubeck to keep time / 181
maybe a mantra / 183
father's day / 185
resumé / 188
the day job / 192
elegy for the american dream / 194
a cheeseburger on memorial day/ 196
on finding three hundred dollars in a book
   on FDR that I ordered off the internet / 197
a fedora and a mustache / 198
kerouac go home / 199
wonder bread, chipped ham, tastycakes / 201
postcard from jeanette pennsylvania / 203
beckemeyer illinois 1958 / 205
new eagle pennsylvania 1960 / 207
a palomino and a bull snake / 209
beauty is a rare thing / 210
the ballad of dominic ierace / 213
wishing rain on muskingum county / 215
postcard from blue ash / 216
molotov party / 218
these waters were dry / 220
the confederate general of osage county / 222
thunder alley / 223
getting any feed for your chickens? / 224
breakfast in 1974 / 226
postcard from the flint hills / 228

the dust bowl again / 229
postcard from ruidoso / 230
kick at the sky / 231
seventy-three miles from the state line / 232
it was a golden time / 233
climbing trees into arkansas / 234
blind into leaving / 236
from a motel 6 / 238

Jason Baldinger: Guardian of the Slanted Hallway

If you are reading this, then it is safe to say that I have a little bit of your attention. Sure, you have got this book in your hands, but do you have a drink nearby? No? Well go grab you one, your choice but I recommend a High Life. No hurry, I'll wait, because some of the best times and conversations that I've had were while having a drink with friends. Smoke 'em? Sure, if you got 'em, and if you're holding edibles to chew, then chew away.

Now, like when most good memories are shared, someone will write or say *one time*, or *this one time,* or *I remember, do you remember,* and then the story begins . . . . you read the words of past days or hear them, and they are absorbed into the ears or through the eyes sliding through the given paths towards the sensory systems like drifters, like stray dogs looking for a bone, and when found, the magic unfolds to spark a lightning show in our brain's sky.

Once all that magic and jazz has happened, all that is left is to simply enjoy the show.

With that said, I have got several good memories with the man who has written the words within this book, like the Friday night in October 2016 when I finally met him for the first time in the basement of a bookstore in Blue Springs, Missouri.

He had been on tour reading his poetry throughout several states and that night was his last stop before heading back to Pittsburgh, Pennsylvania.

I remember thinking to myself that night, that if there was a person sitting in this crowd who doubted the power of poetry, there was no way they were getting out of the room without a few beautifully placed bruises, because the lineup was eight poets deep and every single one of them were throwing knockout punches from different angles. It was truly something for the ages.

For myself, there have been many more, *one time*, or *this one time*, or *I remember, do you remember,* moments throughout the years with Jason.

Like . . . I remember after a long, cold rainy drive in 2017 to read poems at the Jawbone Festival in Kent, Ohio, we made the drive over to Jason's apartment the following day for the first of many readings at the White Whale Bookstore. Afterwards we had drinks at the BBT and it was the first time being introduced to the slanted hallway, which I find to be truly an epic treasure.

Then there was the time after a long, long night of drinking and eating Gus's World Famous fried chicken and bbq ribs at a kitchen table in Belle, Missouri, that we woke up and made our way to a bookstore in St. Louis, Missouri, for another great night of reading poetry.

And who could forget about the time after a reading and book release for Jason's latest book at the Brillobox in Pittsburgh when I stepped outside of his apartment to smoke a cigarette and passed out on the stoop. Waking up around 3a.m., I watched a young couple across the street making love against a telephone pole. They had no clue that I was there, and I had no clue yet that I had been accidently locked out and would sleep the rest of the early morning away in the backseat of my car. That moment, like so many other moments made its way into a poem, as it should have. Later that day we all traveled to Cleveland, Ohio.

Do you remember when several poets spent a weekend in a huge house on Iron Avenue in Salina, Kansas, for The Heart of the Heartland Poetry Festival? I do, and of course, Jason was one of those poets.

I could go on and on sharing memories, many more readings with Jason and friends at the White Whale Bookstore, Venessa's release party, snow falling as we had dinner that would rival any Thanksgiving Day spread at Stinky's Bar . . . that is of course if good bar food is your idea of Thanksgiving.

I guess that the point that I'm trying to make is this, Jason Baldinger has become one of the very few people that I truly cannot imagine living this crazy life without. He's a helluva poet, a genuine soul, a dear friend, a brother.

I once wrote:

"Some people are chewed up and swallowed whole by cities, others unhinge their jaws and swallow cities for the nourishment of their own survival. Reading Jason Baldinger, I was reassured of what I already believed to be true — Baldinger is Pittsburgh poetry and will always survive. He has his city and so many others flowing through his veins. His poems are maps constantly unfolding to navigate the streets between the head and the heart he possesses. This collection will take you high, drop you low, and then pick you back up again. It's Baldinger at his best, opening up the car door and inviting you to climb in. Sit back, relax and enjoy. You have a damn fine ride ahead."

To me, that blurb is still quite relevant, especially to this book that you are holding in your hand right now.

This book is a collection of poems spanning a decade. These poems were hand selected by Jason himself, they're poems that will take you on a trip, traveling with a man who will show you his own *one time,* or *this one time,* or *I remember, do you remember* moments, and trust me, they are moments that will stick with you, moments that pack a punch. . .you just might even notice a few new beautifully placed bruises on yourself. And if so, I can probably speak for Jason when I tell you, you're goddamn welcome.

Well, my High Life is empty. Turn the page and enjoy what is ahead . . .

a great fucking book!

                - Victor Clevenger, Carrollton, Missouri, 2-20-21

you're a poor thief you're leaving
all your diamonds behind

-bob weir
Cottonwood Lullaby

(but where is what I started for so long ago?
and why is it yet unfound?)

-walt whitman
Facing West From California Shores

utopia

we leave it all behind
shut off the grid
escape the nineteenth century
build a mansion
on these banks ohio
create our great society
with a nod to edward bellamy

one hundred men and women
true believers
on a quest for harmony
on a quest to commune
as spiritual beings
find our true souls
our real lives

everyone working together
to enrich the group
in this righteous way
we'll show this rattled world
there is peace, there is serenity

we build this heaven
to understand our earth
we have no ears to hear
the words of a modern world

tonight, our task complete
we celebrate our future
we dance while december
night rain glowers
all the fury of god

we boast of our new world
laugh at fools who fail to pardon our grace

the ohio rises

we are sure that this new world
will insulate us from harm

the ohio rises

we are the shining example
now let the world see

the ohio rises
the ohio crushes these walls
the water sweeps us away

tonight, the new world has died
the ocean ohio
washes our found lives away

new straitsville, sunday october 17

sunday morning
god's garden
fall hangs in sunlight
trees burst full color

mexicali jesus
wild irish rose
and a temperamental
power steering pump
have nothing to say

the black diamond region
open, stretched
a history of backroads
a history in scars

gears grind away ghosts
reality enamel thin
iron works, brick kilns

the reverend chain smokes
black asphalt traces
wind here to candytown
onto new pittsburgh
onto jobs
then to new straitsville

a dog chases an atv down main
lunch counters fall from pez dispensers
topped with samuel gompers death mask

sunday in appalachia
southern style buffet
laid out in newsprint

this town's smudged headlines
shout how these humans burned
shout how this land burned
shout how these people struggled
for better lives in the shadow
of the colossus of capital failed

they shout for this town
built up, now crumbling down

windber

these beatnik girls
spill bohemian glory
on the coppertops of bars
we fire drinks back
faster than we fill then
still there are no pink elephants for me

sun splinters hotel windows
birds chitter august songs
delirium tremens in a sleeping bag
shaking on a concrete floor

three hours out
shrieks stab slumber
I stumble downstairs
to find the commotion

an old drunk woman
after bare floor communion
lost the ability to keep
blood under her skin

arroyos fill
blood from broken noses
stains linoleum, stains carpets

I am useless to these moments
a drunk is poor solace to a drunk
blood is a clumsy dance partner

I scutter back to my room
sleep to scuttle this lifetime hangover
damn the squeal of blood sermons

today, I am rattled sleepless
destined instead to stumble
toward morning sun
a knife sticking behind my ear

I'm destined to climb
train track mountains
survey the town of johnny weissmuller
survey the town of alan freed
while rattling chains
for the ghost of american diners

sunday church services soothe me
hymns crawl to the street
ashamed of their gift of tongues
I stand toward the back
shout a prayer for the faithful

for a shower and clean shirt
I'll believe any lie you say
I'll sing to any god
that will grant me
acetaminophen

we all seek earthly peace
there is no peace here
I return to the street
dry as a vampire

on main I scavenge
for a greasy spoon
to wrestle this hangover
to spell penance
to bless with relief

I am the merriwether lewis
of the laurel highlands
I've shot bears in my sleep

today, my suicide note is blank
this town has been erased
maps keep no record this existed
a history of backroads misplaced
but there's gotta be a diner here someplace

life with lions

at the edge of his bed
I realize calling him a son of a bitch
changes nothing. I have no reasons to forgive
damn or apply any quality of mercy
the years make things different

he's upright
hospital lights highlight
mouth drooping left
hollowed barrel chest
skin a tent for loose bones
bloodstained hands i.v tattooed
face a disparate clash of mother and father
        now tearing apart

the way we know he hears
is heart rate, ekg spikes
spires of life fading

we've spoken two sentences in twelve years
still, he's the closest to a father I had
even when he was closest
there was nothing more holding us in place
than the tenuous tether of family

that tether snapped
after stretching thin

through his lifetime of addiction

now I have my own lifetime
my own addictions

there is nothing here worth damning
burning or blaming

we all share our life with lions
we'll all be traveling salesmen when we die

holy ghost (for amir)

1958
kids in cleveland
grow up on streets
that border black neighborhoods
that border polish neighborhoods
they all go to school together
no thoughts of color

summertime
summertime is different
nobody goes into someone else's neighborhood
unless they're looking for a fight
not necessarily because they're black
not because they're polish
because it's turf
space in the city
HA!

so, these black kids
sneak down early friday morning
sneaking so those polish kids
won't catch them getting
a donut, a danish, a bearclaw
they sneak then hightail it back
a short cut through the park
you can't see what's invisible baby

those black kids know
they've crossed space time continuums
they've crossed manmade boundaries
when they see albert ayler
perched between brownstones
between black and polish neighborhoods
honkin' and wailin' and honkin' and squealin'
andhonkinandwailinandsquealinandhonkinandwailin
loving the bounce back echo
reverberation mixes with horns and traffic
and city sounds and breaking glass
and rock pelting off walls thrown by polish kids
who hated the noise and it mixes
with husbands and wives yelling to shut up
and birds and colors and traffic and whatever sound
bleeding through time
it was *cosmic*

it was cosmic, man

albert took note of nothing but sound

it was cosmic

folks called him holy ghost

dead man's hymn

after seven bars
one near brawl
we swerve to his car

he starts to throw up
first thought to catch
it one cupped hand
thinks better of it
reaches for a half empty
mcdonald's cup on the dash

vomits into it
doesn't spill a drop
I pull over
he sets cup on curb
wipes hands in dead leaves
wipes face on his sleeve

back in the passenger seat
we make for his car
he speeds home   alive

I find another bar   alive
wrap myself around a stool
drunk cheshire cat
whiskey stripes show
I sing a dead man hymn

berkman

alexander berkman
at the 11th avenue grayhound station
buys a ticket with a .38

hands sweat, brow knit
exasperated
a bus will take you
anywhere you wanna go today

maybe this isn't pittsburgh
maybe history's demarcation
has jumbled steel mill smog
into tech centers that wobble
on cobblestone streets

the workers of the world can still unite
behind the actions of one man
can that man find history
roused from bookishness
to sharpen his tongue
stir the proletariat to rise again

as the storm gathers
there's port authority
to keep him dry
there's horse drawn cabs
drivers hum *camptown races*

as they chase the little bill's ghost
up the mon into a valley forgotten
a valley of past lives and old ways

berkman realizes it's raining soot
snowing soot, even as july
sits with an ice block in front of the fan
his fingers sweat, familiarize themselves with steel

can you really *take* a human life?
can a man extinguish a spirit's fire
like a coke furnace? can one man
slow the bessemer process
once they recognize the wolf at their door

steel infrastructure rots
once stained with human blood
that blood runs from uptown
through the south side
to rest in homestead
at the end of a pinkerton's rifle

there are so may pittsburgh's
the one la belle riviera ran through
before they collared her mississippi

there's the pittsburgh
that cracks like art blakey's snare
one that captures perfect, one shot
the one that sways loose, fierce
as bop blares along wylie avenue

there's the pittsburgh
the wolves devoured
the one left as rust belt carcass
the one rotting in western pennyslvania smog

there is pittsburgh reborn
taking hospitals and tech jobs
after years a spinster

berkman watches it all
building built, demolished
workers employed, then unemployed
he hears uncle andy tell frick
they'd both meet in hell someday

he hopes that someday comes
faster than the exit velocity
of a josh gibson home run
faster than the collective memory
flickers out of a city of workers
that never did unite behind one man

berkman daydreams
down fifth avenue
time stopped
thousand frozen, window shop
oblivious to the wolves waiting

they're petty bourgeois
lulled passive

everything they need on credit
except a living wage
except universal health insurance

berkman remembers
crossing the bridge of sighs
ross street shadowed in gaslight

berkman thinks back
allegheny city, birmingham
merge with this city
a host for an industry
that feeds on broke back hunkies
who walk streets between mills and bars
then home for troubled sleep
before returns to relief rolls
they are deadly aware
of the wolves outside their doors

berkman understands
there is no second mortgage on a cell
solitary is only a summer home
where time is spent reflecting
on the consequence of wounding a figurehead
but the workers of the world
will unite behind the actions of one man

berkman enters a crystal palace
hands sweat profusely
outside shoppers shop in still frame

workers work in still frame
machines hum a deafening
shrill *camptown races*

there is a wolf at the door
mahogany swings wide
.38 floats into slippery hands

three shots
then struggle
blade shines
there is the tangled limbs
there is blood
and these dreams
of workers to be treated as human
will not be deferred any longer

the workers of the world
can unite behind the actions of one man

alexander berkman is in chains
as he crosses the bridge of sighs

the proletariat is in chains
as they cross the bridge of sighs

sarah anne

sarah anne
your eyes are a bend in the creek
where we see
all the way to charleston

sarah anne
why don't we settle into a quiet
couple of acre life
we'll ride tractors in circles

sarah anne
the years are nothing more than
your grandma's plastic trinkets
my father's cuff links and wedding rings

sarah anne
on saturday nights
we'll build a church
that we alone can burn down

sarah anne
on sunday mornings
we'll worship in the finest corner bar

sarah anne
when the supermarket folds
we'll live on fish our children
catch with their teeth

sarah anne
the post office is a trailer park
our mail is pony express

sarah anne
when you forge my signature
don't dot the i's
with little suns, hearts or flowers

sarah anne
watch the tipple lights
those lights are a shield
to keep the world away

sarah anne
with the sun nested in your hair
your wrist brace and a can of diet coke
you are forever nineteen

sarah anne
on summer nights
we'll move the tv to the porch
watch until well after dark

sarah anne
the dog is dead
we buried him
on the far side of the road

sarah anne
god may be dead
we move like locust through here

betty

in-between jobs
stop home for a sandwich
my mom follows me to my bedroom
tells me my grandfather died
a massive heart attack
he went to sleep
never woke up

I'm not shocked
he was mid seventies
a large man who said often
I've spilled more whiskey
than you'll ever drink

we were years from
endless saturday morning drives
watch sun up
from a job site

sometimes we trade emotion for bravery
sometimes it's hard to make something real

I didn't know what to do with myself
I decide to work my next shift
save bereavement time for tomorrow

I call the job I just finished
between bites of sandwich
my boss sam is on vacation

betty, sam's assistant, answers
I tell betty my grandfather passed
I can't make it in wednesday
I'll be back friday

betty is not sorry for my loss
she doesn't dish out sympathy
betty scoffs
betty tells me I can't call off

betty's husband passed away two months ago
betty got two weeks off, flowers for the funeral
no one said a word when betty was overwhelmed
excusing herself to the back room

betty's scoff tells me working wednesday
taking meat wrapped in plastic out of boxes
to put meat wrapped in plastic into a cooler
is more important than my goodbye to my grandfather

betty is a good american
she forgets the kindness of others
it's only what have you done for me lately

I tell betty that no matter what
I won't be in on wednesday
if she has a problem she can call sam
I hang up

now I am furious
betty, quite frankly, is a bitch

wednesday passes
I carry my grandfather's casket
uphill
I continue to be brave
until my uncle
my grandfather's only surviving son
breaks down

they lower the casket
I break down
we all howl
wild dogs full of human grief

friday morning comes
I drive to work
consider how I should handle
the betty situation

I get there on time
sit in my car for ten extra minutes
let my anger come

almost to the backroom door
sam shoots out
oh good! you're here!

fuck you, I'm out!
sam is confused
I toss smock, name badge at him
walk for the front door

he stammers
sad he will unpack meat wrapped in plastic
then put meat wrapped in plastic into a cooler

sam yells
STOP!

what?

can I ask why?

ask betty!

ray

ray worked the diaper factory
salt and pepper hair
salt and pepper beard
he did mechanic work
managed his own line

ray was charming
all the old ladies loved ray
all the women my age
weren't creeped out
when ray gave them a hug
pecked them on the cheek
and called them sweetie

it's after christmas
ray hasn't been to work in days
employees whisper in every corner
gossip, how much ray drinks
at least a case a day

we're called to a meeting
we hear ray passed away

afterward lunchroom gossip
a holiday with no one
to celebrate
an empty case

ray took his belt
tied it the basement rafters
kicked out his chair

suddenly
all ray's loneliness
slipped away

the hymn to toilet duck

we got two to four trucks a night
forty-eight or fifty-three foot trailers
wobbly box castles, dangerous merch mazes
it wasn't unusual to grab a box and avalanche
free from gravity we all fall down

this particularly humid night
soaked to the skin
in a metal box baked in all day sun
I lift a box of paper towels
as I let it down, another box
comes straight for my head
no escape
a victim of gravity

normal reaction
throw up hands
but I blew out the ligaments in my wrist
last year in a similar situation
hell, it was better than a broken jaw

this subterfuge box
toilet duck if memory serves
scores a direct hit to my temple
I'm winded, I'm fading
stagger back
bounce off metal wall

perception spirals
room swings left then right
everything dims
I fold
drop to the floor
dazed

my manager, next down the line
asks if I'm alright
I don't know

I get my wind, slowly up
unpacking gingerly
everything swims
this fickle reality

I finish shades of pale
keep working till six, nauseous
I ask to leave early, warn the manager
I may have a concussion
he sends me home
he doesn't insist on a hospital

I drive with non-existent reactions
stop signs walk away from me
lost on side streets for a thousand years
finally find my driveway
exit the car not sure how I got here
leave the keys in the car
have to find them when
I can't unlock the apartment door

I leave a note
to be woken up
answer basic questions
I'm not supposed to sleep
fucking christ I'm tired

twelve hours later
finally make the hospital
dizzy and confused, I stop at work
to get paperwork so they cover the bills
manager on duty rubs my head, *poor boy*

there's gotta be an easier way to get a day off

my three days as an environmentalist

2000
computers were supposed to end the world
non-existent recessions brought stolen
elections, then very real recessions
winter came early with a brooks brothers riot
thanksgiving, I went to work for the sierra club

first night, I shadow the boss
a housing plan in cranberry
we knocked on doors, middle management
housewives tossed us money in hope
we could save those dear endangered wolves

we made quota by 7, the night was cooling
we knocked on one last door, middle age couple
invite us in, offer us dinner, offer us wine
we talked wolves and stolen elections
all sorts of bleeding-heart things
it was a perfect first day
I looked forward to more days saving wolves
days talking about saving the world

monday in dormont
pleasant fall chill now winter blast
wandering streets, knocking on doors
half-finished speeches, doors slam
FUCK OFF!

up and down half mile hills
warm up breaks in a rite-aid
scrape change for candy bar
first night solo, I make my quota
last house of the night
lady with four kids felt pity
handed me thirty-five bucks
as she changed her youngest

day two
knock knock
hi, I'm with sierra club
out here today raising
money to save wolves

stained wife beater replies
why the fuck should I give you money
for wolves, FOR FUCKING WOLVES
I lost my FUCKING job
I ain't got shit
how the fuck and I gonna buy my kids
CHRISTMAS PRESENTS? Are WOLVES
gonna buy MY FUCKING KIDS CHRISTMAS PRESENTS?
FUCK YOU AND YOUR FUCKING WOLVES!

the doors got no better
I spent most of the night in rite-aid
buying candy bars, change dwindling
ears sour from doorbells

day three
nobody answers their door
there's an apb out
liberals are looking for your money

I wander around rite-aid
no money for candy bars
trying to keep my toes from turning blue
boss checks in at 7
there's two hours left for quota
if I don't make it she'll let me go

I knock
I knock
no answer

laid off at the end of my shift
borrow a five for cigarettes
parking is free if I can wait till 11

the hymn at the end

it's a mediocre day to be fired
snow, mostly flurries
it's been four years
since the last unemployment
everything is more complicated
everything feels like suffocating
this is how I identified myself for years

she asks through wires
what I'm going to do next
she might have meant the big next
all I could think of was leaving
driving, motion on motion

three hours later in erie
pass a sign the wind had its way with
we sell blow
I stand shorelines
cigarette smoke, snow flakes
defeated

fucking game is rigged
give your soul, you will be asked for more
eat shit, you will be asked to eat more
repeat until you're too old to care
then please die

speeding home, I've got nothing
I won't want to talk when she gets home
rather forget than rehash

answering machine lights
condolence blinks

*hey brother this is rob. I just wanted to let
you know that when they told me they fired you
I decided I'd had enough of this shit!
I handed in my keys, said fuck them
walked out. I'm at the cage
have a drink with me!*

beep
*hey its james. when I walked in they told
me what happened, I thought about what a pile of shit
this is. I fucking quit!. I'm at the cage.
I just bought rob a drink, you're next*

beep
*hey it's gary. I stuck around until they sent me to the bank
I couldn't deal with it anymore. I almost got to the bank,
then I saw rob and james in the cage laughing. the whole
thing pissed me off. I went back without doing the
banking. I called her a bitch and stormed out. I'm at the
cage with rob and james. heather followed me out too.*

beep
rob, plastered, unintelligible
I barely make out his voice
jukebox yelling, he's sorry
they're heading home
then he thanked me

the ballad of mickey mantle

in rochester, hotel bars are full
wedding guests, women in spring colors
their drunk laughter sounds like poodles
their beaus, loosen ties, camp along bar rails
fire down jameson shots

pittsburgh is on the phone
momo, the bartender
overhears me say *birthday*
her eyes light, she mouths *birthday*
I shake my head no, but there's a free beer
on the bar in seconds

she asks what whiskey I take
I remind her it's not my birthday
but jim beam black
she pours two, shoots with me

I hear poodles
momo rolls her eyes
I think of the border guard laughing
when I said I'd rather drive
through ontario than ohio
he asked why, I fired back
did you ever fucking drive across ohio?

thankfully he laughed
I thought I'd sealed myself for an ordeal
crossing borders has never been easy

one groomsman, tie around his head
saddles up for a drink, claps me on the back
buys me a shot, *happy birthday!*

evidently momo told everyone
it's my birthday, she hustles free alcohol
I'm not complaining
drunk is better than sitting alone
sinking into an endless king size bed

strange memories flick across bourbon
new york is a weird frame of mind
circle an inventory of motel nights
strung out in albany
fuming in peekskill
broken in lake placid
all those alien nights in nameless towns
where the headless horsemen wasn't really undead

another shot in front of me
guy who orders it, his girlfriend
leans on me, she whispers thick
almost in my ear, *it's your birthday?*

I've lost the ability to focus
in blurred lights I catch glimpses
john brown's white shock ghost

I slur to momo, cash me out
scrawl a tip that's double the check
momo says *happy birthday!*

I crawl on my fists across navy carpets
bridesmaids, wedding guests shout *happy birthday!*
we tip closer to blackout

last thought as darkness comes real
smoking cigarettes with a surly canada goose
the hudson valley finds fall
I'm almost frederick exley lost

my head at dawn ripe as a sewer
true death is the only reward to be found
I check out, no sleep wedding guests
once again wish me *happy birthday!*

ignition
a friend calls, he's getting married
press accelerator, head east for cooperstown

I feel stoned, out of sorts, nasty
in a way only mickey mantle could be proud of

hymn to free's *fire and water*
(for matt spolar)

new hampshire
refuses roads
squeezes into afternoon gray

I drag low between rail car diners
crawl inside a junk shop
pale myriad ways to match the sky
debate buying an lp by free

in bars hidden in basements
empty bottles spring time loose
there's a pool table dissertation
on boston's post hardcore scene
to bore afternoon to evening
I field calls, set my path
waste some last days boogie

matt is on his way
fresh from a yellow fever shot
renee on his arm
if she puts out the sun
he has light bulbs in his pockets

we wander rearrangements
long bar room shadows
virgil is here, his spirit anyhow

we remember pittsburgh streets
in the clarity of nostalgia

both of us have strayed
far enough now to know
home is a four letter word

summer washes down
stars shine through bathroom doors
the universe takes notes
on abandoned burrito wrappers

an alley, a halfway house
the oldest building in town
built puritanical in blue smoke
george washington slept here

2am, a free record plays
oh, I wept
turntable spins lost grooves
riffs hang on the night
another planet

the space between chords
where paul rodgers teaches
angels to sing

renee asleep
matt altered
reads the *lady pittsburgh* to me

his heart now a hole
tears fall though
pittsburgh is too far away
home is never any closer

a victim of expansion
these substances compound dreams
past lives when a moose
chased me out of roadside woods
unhappy that I was marking its territory

still life panic, dick in hand
hold my pants up
try not to piss on myself
I scutter up the embankment

I found safety
but every rock in the white mountains
laughed and laughed and laughed

I swear to you now
in this unmoored state
if I saw that moose in a bar
that could be anywhere
that could be home
I'd belly that bar
buy that son of a bitch moose
its next goddamn round

I came up empty

indianapolis walks naked
out of a motel room
onto an indiana beach
tucked between
an indiana chemical plant
and an indiana power plant

no one noticed
she was another constellation
in a sky boredom couldn't raise

I check my pulse
watch cemeteries
wear headstones for centuries
I come up empty

I replace tail lights
with every mile route 50 eats
I come up empty

mostly, I drift listless
along great dull plains
think of ernie pyle
and the midwest wind
sad   dusty   beautiful

listen as it wears itself out
with each gust of each generation

gone

the old weird america

highway 61
endless iowa fields
you never see over the stalks
to find a lost blue sky sea
to find a lost green unripe sea

this lost nation earth
anything that shines
garners the limits of attention

afternoon sun rests
on mosaic stations of the cross
on sculpture tributes to freedom

this pottery reflects
light through space

rub eyes clear
of dumb road haze
the old weird america
just said grace

I am rain

on a balcony
over jackson square
sippin' gin and tonic

an older couple from dallas
sing the katrina lament
ain't no wave
no gust of wind
gonna hold my body down

we roar with naked women
mermaids float across mardi gras night
congo square blares, wild tchoupitoulas
marie laveau's bones keep french quarter rhythm

bourbon street pirates bang out boogie woogie
banjos play jazz vulgar as it was born
a five hundred pound black man
swims across aqua marine walls
belts *saint james infirmary*
ready his coffin
I'll shoot dice for pallbearer

a tulane waitress from houston
lines up abita and whiskey chasers
she charges me for the odds

quartet rips hard bop
fierce roots, savage teeth
buddy bolden's *funky butt*
conjures on steam

three am zombies hold a tropical storm by the wings
I'm breathless, rolling, a big river across levees
this neon glory

dixie diner hamburgers
glow in drunk diamond hands
I need an anchor in jukebox lights

speakers cough classic craft
bobby marchan, ernie k-doe
lee dorsey, alan toussaint
if I hear frankie ford
I'll lose my fucking mind

dumaine at royal
corner of charters
not on as far as decatur
summer is helpless
I am rain dying
in this swamp air

BLACKOUT

dreams fall easy
red fades the devil
I walk on gilded splinters

faulkner writes soldiers pay
with *dippermouth blues*
endless in his head

andrew jackson fights
johnny horton over the rights
the ballad of new orleans

a windshield covered in leeches
mannequin alligators in red velvet
dresses swing hips across storyville

irma thomas lights prayer candles
to appease that motherfucker sun
pigeons dust off rented beignets

captain america
tell me when we get our asses
to the other side of pontchartrain

ballad of forty mosquitos

cypress tree swamps
surround fort king george
I sing the ballad of forty mosquitos
keep my chest moving
bugs will have no respite
I've been warned they will exsanguinate
a human if given two minutes

I spy ancient dragons, swamp monsters
through windows of resurrection moss
evidence the south faked adaptation

mothers day in valdosta
armies of taffeta and polyester
trail between sunday services
and the lunch buffet at o'neals

I pass a dying desoto
radio commercials crackle
walls of automatic weapons
we can't afford to lose our freedom

wait, what freedom are we referring to?

in andersonville, one hundred and fifty years ago
forty-five thousand men lived in a square mile
with one spring for toilet, bath and drinking

passive earthworks full of crows and ghosts
fences constructed, shebangs vacant
this wind of lice carries only sorrow

radio and history converge
captain henry wirz was hanged for treason
at a time when all men committed treason
he hanged for thirteen thousand dead
as he swings from a noose of resurrection moss
it's clear that war hasn't ended

one hundred and fifty years of bodies
four hundred years of bodies
while we celebrate the wrong men
for all that blood spilled
humans are not free

radio crackles
messages to backwoods georgia
I wonder when it will play an ad that asks
are any of us truly free?

this ornate melancholy rises
rain clouds across west georgia
will break in alabama downpours

lonely crossroads pass
empty as our freeborn lives
these last color splashes
this lonely georgia sunset

these days of heaven

in the land of flowers
at the heels of conquistadors
not looking for eternal youth
looking for america

among churches and forts
older than the day I forgot my name
squirrels wrestle in royal palm
lizards fire across the trail
heat lightning on the ground
armadillos on a radar range
alligators gawked by tourists
who say *here* in english
they flash photos amazed
in german, french and japanese

I will never doubt mosquitos again
I carry their blood, which may be my blood
communion stories in welts rising
across the everglades through shark valley
into the big cypress where at panther
crossings I wait for reeds to move
where are the big cats of our imagination?
where is the sky, I want to keep it in my pocket?

it's a typical night in bradenton
redneck princesses in daisy dukes and high heels

serve cubanos in deli dives
picnic benches and highlife for everyone

across the street a ball game starts
star spangled prayers, the first pitch
home team loss followed by fireworks

on the hood of my car
flashback in neon bursts
vasovagal visions of the lady florida
in a dress of palm frond and hibiscus
she says, *you've found america*
now can you find your soul?

II

it's one of those days where nothing materializes
you move
        and move
                and move
the windshield is forever
the love bugs hit like rain drop
                     drop
                        drop

in cemeteries, turtles sleep on stones
at the roadside, the turkey vultures get lazy

these days
        these days
                so sleepy

the windshield is forever
I'm twenty miles from tampa
    twenty miles from williston
    twenty miles from hernando
    twenty miles from archer
    twenty miles from gainesville
    twenty miles from the terminus of fucking forever

there is nothing
not a dusty bookshop
or a diner or a burger king
where everyone is too bored to exist

these days heat rises slow
highway vanishes under haze
stare off forever
through a windshield

these days of heaven
these days *are* heaven

the windshield is forever

back when we were wild

kansas
I wish we could share a kiss
but the prairie sneaks up
so goddamn fast
then never leaves

three wasted days
boiling in hundreds heat
across endless flats
with a mute ghost

I haven't seen a hill
somehow I missed
a famous frontier town

I'm reading ray carver
while I drive
seems more useful
than a map

in a junk shop
or a motel
with no hot water
I catch a smell
that reminds me
of atonement
of another time
back when we were wild

the museum club

off the wagon
the museum club
flagstaff arizona

pronghorns stare down
from the heaven side
of the bar

lone star beer
another- another- another
mamacita painted with nipples out
guides to the piss trough

amble back to bar stool wobble
trischa, this victoria is for you!
here's to your first night on the job

spill me stories of your little boy
remind me again of snow
how there are new words
for it when it falls in may

here's to latin night racing by
so you can dig into to this new routine
I'll be here scribbling notes
on mountain lions
stalking their prey
in the dance floor dark

the grand canyon is a platter of deviled ham
tourists wander stadium size parking lots
agape in american wonder
oblivious to havasupai tears

my heart leaps out of my chest
into a bright angel morning
uriah heep rises out of the colorado
easy living

this is easy living tonight
bar in full swing
cross the dance floor again
ducking tractor beams
the orbit of booty

lost in the trees
I toss my garter up to a call girl
laugh as chicano cowboys
hats over their eyes
mumble into bud light
I am a gringo

some biker has issues
he doesn't want to be left
as the last white man in this bar
he shouts as I leave, *pussy*
I really don't care

goodbye pacific ocean blue

storm clouds
puffed with purpose
sing, *goodbye pacific ocean blue*

blues hang on oregon
a cloak of rain
a cutlass of drizzle
donuts dipped in rainwater
taste sweeter than the sea

kids smoke pot outside motel door
they say *awkward* as I leave for beer
I should charge a joint for the real estate

their tiny chatter voices
turn to stoned deserts
when mixed with screeches of karaoke journey
we are all mongrels in a long past dead america

down burnside, illusions paint
in strip bars and street lights
I write a flood of dreams on the back of my hand

last night I dreamt of a wizard's hat and green knights
last night I dreamt of crystalline moose of loving grace
last night I dreamt of crater lake snows higher than clouds
last night I dreamt I wasn't the drunkest man in redmond
last night I dreamt water was my imagination

I woke up listening
harsh elemental whirl
motel air conditioner

I remembered spending my last fifty cents
on a slot machine, one last attempt
to win bus fare *anywhere* it wasn't cold

zen and the western sunset

leaning into a bowl of tortilla soup
in a town called priest lake
where there's barely enough business
to be called a district
barely enough people here
to still call this a town

I'm the only one here
the waiter sits down
says when he and his wife
opened this place they had forty
people on staff. now his wife
cooks, he plays handyman, waits
tables when the other girl is off

he was an east coast kid
who never felt right in city noise
back in the eighties when the economy
carter could take credit for
went right back in the shitter
with reagan's austerity
he had enough, headed west
through the texas oilfields

he made money, met his wife
neither of them were happy
so they quit, wandered till they found idaho

he became a mortgage broker
she bought this place

it was a good living
he got tired of bullshit
burying people in mortgages
so, he left that too
he and his wife get by alright
but the whole damn dream is dying

anyone here with a lick of sense
bailed when the lumber mill automated
most headed for the north dakota oil boom

hell, if they could sell this place
he and his wife would hit the road
see it all over again
one hundred and fifty miles at a time

what can I tell him?
things fall apart
may be trite, but it's true
sometimes it all falls apart perfect
leaving you nowhere
with nothing
only
zen and a western sunset

hymn to the immaculate heart of mary

(for jon and pam)

this bar window offers
an excellent view of sunset
if I turn a bit I catch
sun between domes
of the immaculate heart of mary

if I hadn't quit smoking
this would be the perfect moment
as I reflect on my homecoming
try to order fragments of memory
into novels i'll write two sentences at a time

all of this is fleeting
this dusted purple sky
this backlit blue bar smoke
this cold oberon, I peel the label
wait for my housemate, his girlfriend

they paw each other
play grabass, flip jukebox selections
big star's *o, dana* then *kizza me*
stray sam cooke song
bowie then the undertones
before x-ray spex
thank fucking god no *marquee moon*

pawing graduates to making out
buzzcocks' *ever fallen in love*
shambles in the speakers
this song and sweet's *fox on the run*
are parameters which fill out my existence

they are touchstones of reality
they prove this bar is and that I am
I always hear them here
that makes me sure
I'm in pittsburgh
for the first time in months

I miss this place more upon returning
the newness of familiarity
leaves me innocent

I'm happy to be back
to shoot pool with no effort
to cash out only to head
to another bar for a twelve pack
before I sink into the couch
drunk focus on neil young and devo
o, this grainy vhs beerlight!

hymn to inevitability

she was sixteen, full of middle america dreams
her path was clear she'd be married
then barefoot, then pregnant
that was in her head when we met

three months later, christmas in view
she insisted our engagement
was the only thing she wanted
it was inevitable

at eighteen I knew the world was bigger than I thought
    it was
I knew the word inevitable should almost never be used
I didn't know that we confuse love for lust
I caved at her behest, with my mother's blessing
it was a pre-engagement, devil in the details

we went ring shopping, sterile mall stores
high markup gaudy jewelry, we didn't know better
layaway plans augment hourly wages under five dollars
    an hour

with the holiday a week away, I had to think
of places, spaces romantic to drop to my knee
ask questions that were inevitable

my family was on their way to my grandfather's
I remembered a mountaintop minutes away
commanding view of cambria county
commanding view of what is slipping away

we drove detours up the mountain
her impatient, not clear on the plan
at the top we talked
I'd only been here once
i hadn't noticed then
this was an illegal trash dump
dead soldiers, laundry machines, car parts
chaise lounges, exhaust pipes
litter the length of the pull-off

my stepfather hides in a tree
video camera stretches across highway
I couldn't change my decision
I find the place with the least trash
drop to one knee
not realizing I'm about to kneel
on a desiccated raccoon corpse

her eyes get bigger, anticipation shouts
I shift my body so she doesn't see
the dead animal between my legs

I pop a catcher's squat
crotch covers the corpse
she says *yes*

my stepfather climbs out of his tree
they walk away, happy chittering birds

I kick the corpse out of spite

sam

sam was from saudi arabia
at least his parents were
sam was born in new york
I never met his parents
but sam sounded like me
his skin was darker
I didn't really care
that sam was different

sam and I worked in big box hell
three to eleven most nights
I worked sporting goods and automotive
sam worked in pets

after work we'd pile in a car
head for eat & park
drink coffee til four
find a parking lot to burn off caffeine
we were too young to drink legally
we didn't care
we wanted to be young
run around all night
there were no consequences
we were a little crazy
chasing that last moment
right before responsibility got hold

one night riding with sam
in his parent's minivan
sam's doing donuts
sam's doing neutral drops
we're having fun
no traffic around
no one's hurting anyone

cops directed traffic near ongoing construction
a cruisers rolls down
lights on tongue out in the dark
sam pulled over

the cop realized sam was an arab
sam tried to remain polite in gruff accusation
sam remained polite as the cop
opened the door
ripped sam out
tossed him head first
into the side of the van
called sam a *sand nigger*
somehow I'd never heard those words together before

cop's partner shines light in my eyes
do I have a problem?
already seasoned by a few run-ins with cops
nod my head no
drop my hat over my eyes

sam in an arm bar
while the cop's partner
writes a ticket
sam remains polite
never cries out
always says *sir*

they let sam go
he has a ticket
a heavy fine and a sore arm

I apologize as we drive
still not sure what to do
sam is less concerned about the cops
more about his parents, the ticket

we rode in silence to get coffee
no one needed to explain
this system points out differences
maybe we wouldn't notice otherwise

I lost track of sam
I lost track of everyone from that summer
those seasonal lessons stay with me

hymn to grease

10:30
breakfast mcdonalds smell
switches
to lunch mcdonalds smell

ear infection no better
it came with an upper respiratory infection
a few weeks ago
lungs rattle regular now

I barely function
been out of work months
shit hasn't gotten serious
it's coming

I had a panic attack the other night
edge of the bed
short gulps of air
almost an hour
girlfriend insisted on a hospital
I declined

full minutes explanations
aversions to hospital bills
forged by a six thousand dollar ER visit

ten years
of bills for paper hats
send a ten spot check monthly
the reality of no insurance

today I'm talking to mcdonalds
about the management program
sip a small coke
hand over my mouth
to keep dry heaves down
every question answered to myself first
do not vomit

mcdonalds asks another question
deep breathe answers
as grease smell attacks

I think of a girl I dated
she worked at burger king
I'd race her home
we'd race out of clothes
into a shower
trying to wash out that smell

no further questions
he never took note of what I said
I'll get the job
everybody does

I won't show for the shift
not desperate enough...*yet*
silver lining
I never vomited once

the winter of office supplies

the toll of a few rough months totaled
carrying a couch into a new apartment
I hate to stop but I have to take the call
signal to the guy carrying the other arm *take a break*
dig out phone, bark *hello*
take a seat, couch on my lap

after five years together I decided to leave, mid-november
arguments escalating, she'd taken to throwing punches
I blocked, ducked or let her hit my chest
I'd wait 'til she got tired, hold her till she collapsed
neither with much to say

I knew her rage, knew what renewed it
I knew it wasn't me
in these moments she didn't see my face
I tried to get through but there was nothing left
I wasn't helping, I spent my patience

with arrangement to sign a lease
she pleads her case
with another dinner date apology
we try to talk it through
the same story
still, I cave

new year came
I lost my job
spent january on break
february looking for work
march brought illness

no insurance, no doctor
a litany of interviews
eventually smuggled antibiotics
stolen from a vet hospital
thankfully, they weren't beef chewable

she asked me to leave
there was nothing to discuss
I stayed until I found an apartment or a job

next month lost
trying to keep out the house
to avoid the shit and psychic debris
that comes with the end of a relationship

her endless suspicion
as I spent long nights
with concerned friends
she'd call, I'd try talk her down
I couldn't refuse
still needed a place to crash

memorial day
I rushed through six interviews

pulling charm from the depths
my mother scouted apartments
I took a place the landlord
didn't check references
then convinced him to pay security deposits late

it all leads here
six potential jobs
choice six on the phone
I have a couch on my lap
choice six isn't offended
when I bark *hello*
wheeze for wind
accept a job

the winter of office supplies had begun

heaven

in my mid-twenties
when things went sideways
I found myself in elkins west virginia
the last town before those
old mother mountains took over

outside town was a hole in a rock
seen from the highway
cars and microbuses parked in neat lines
jump the fence, skinny down the gulley
there was a beautiful private property waterfall
forty-foot drops, cavern doubling as shallow lake

hippie girls and boys passed joints
kids played in the falls
old people sat on canvas chairs
beautifulandillegalandfree

I returned years later heaven desolate
only to find heaven gone
water dammed
empty holes in rocks
dried muddy stones
lake nothing
nofallsnohippiesnojointsnokids

I wonder to a silent congregation
whether stories
travelsandbedsandbarsandwomenanddrunks
are enough to insulate
when whatever you build comes down
I wonder about life after heaven.

he said only eat half

      these are strong. I ate half
      other half in my pocket
wait on the couch with him, his girlfriend
nurse a beer
wait for alcohol to neutralize
wait for the brownie to hit
wait with saturday night live re-runs

after one, I head home, alcohol
a small buzz, weed not hitting
safe for driving in theory
I make my way down penn ave
              aim for millvale
cross the 40th   it dawns
millvale cops and saturday night
          are a gauntlet to be faced
I think about the dwi I talked myself out of
a few months ago, two beer night
coast through a stop sign, cop let me go, ticket and warning
      after I explained I was two blocks from home

brownie in my pocket, untenable
      I eat the other half   incase

I pass cop cars with video game precision
        tonight, I am perfect
I find my keys, smell the record store smell

        that is my apartment, the other guys apartment
                that is the record store downstairs
the first half of the brownie hits
        zombie wobbles upstairs, through rituals to bed

safe
        tonight, I am perfect

four am, eyes pop open, all of a sudden the room is technicolor, I see every shadow, hear every noise, there is no one to talk to, they (collective or proverbial) were right you don't want a head full of anything when a house gets quiet and dark, I wash my face, careful of the mirror, back to bed, stop for music: amon duul, ash ra temple, terry riley, tiny volume, throbbing sounds, I sink low into mattress, no sleep, a heartbeat

fucking sure

I'm

dying

        we're dying every day, why is it a surprise when you
   feel your
mortality

meditation, how to mark time, sun comes up, lungs of
    daylight fill, I drift, I drift, I drift
this morning I am perfect

asleep

I wake up hours later, legs won't work
I crawl to the bathroom, back to bed
I have to be up in an hour, I have a date at noon

these hour later legs work although my mind a viscous
    place, alcohol hangovers and THC in effect
               they battle for supremacy

breakfast negotiations, greasy, greasy glass eyed, today I
    am not perfect
but I show up on time

it took a month for her to ask why I was weird when I
    arrived

a rabbit from hell

(for steve pellegrino)

I never turn down a mental health day
even when I'm broke
today, I should be a laborer
painting ceilings, patching walls
today, pellegrino has other ideas
he wants to drive the mon valley
he asks me to take notes
while he conjures dead voices

adrift with late morning sun
near joseph yablonsky's centerville clinic
where free medical aid was offered
to struggling UMWA workers to ease the burden
of the black lung the UMWA claimed didn't exist
I see a young boy
no more than eleven
chubby pink turning purple
he runs off the front porch
up a gravel driveway
arms pumping, eyes bulging
a rabbit born from the mouth of hell

the look in his eye says he caught
a glimpse of his future and it terrified him
he swore to god it wouldn't catch him
in a fit of youth, he believed he could escape

the mon valley, poverty, this trailer
all the shackles we as displaced
millionaires believe we can shake

I make a joke something like
that old devil future can't catch me
pellegrino laughs
this is america
the future already caught us

the man who sees underground

eight am, thirteen degrees
keep warm in my car
mike drives up in his backhoe
I hadn't met him before today
he shakes my hand
looks at me through a lazy eye
I'm the man who sees underground
he asks if I've seen bo. maybe bo is a ghost
he'll be dead in less than four months
when kools and iron city turn
his liver into cancer

we chase what the job requires
I return to the warmth of the car
he to the space heater in the cab
the crazy right-wing radio
mike votes outside his interest
I guess I do too

he knocks on the window an hour later
hands me a shovel
I'll start to pull out the fill
I'll need you to move dirt here and there

I stand, top of the hillock
where porch meets the dirt
we yell over diesel

where the standpipe is
how far down is the sewage?
it's the water main that's broken

I'm amazed at the grace
the teeth, the bucket
gentle through dirt
how he sifts through fill
I never imagine poetry
in the use of a front-end loader
he pulls out a bush
lays it on the sidewalk
spent lover
time served

problems manifest
water main runs under sewer line
which runs outside the house
elbows back under the stairs
even a man who sees underground can't anticipate this
he cracks sewer line
I stand ankle deep in shit
we wait for bo

bo arrives
he is not a ghost
he and his kools, mike and his lazy eye
spend the day married couple bickering

shit freezes, I freeze, we freeze
I run jackhammers
muscles have seizures
we spend ten hours with grey skies
we don't feel the cold
we don't feel the dread of the women who will be murdered
we don't feel the cancer coming
we just grunt through shit
watch the backhoe
write poems in steaming dirt

half day hymn

with a powerful urge for fried chicken and collard greens
and a half day vacation I head for carmi's
soul food stops a heart every time

after the feast
with time to kill
                      a little drive
                a little putt putt
          a little pissing around
I take the long way through manchester
the part that died when they cut the expressway in

I take the marshall avenue exit
pass the cemetery my father, his family occupy
pass my mother's childhood home, or the lot, it burned in
    the 80's
pass a tow truck driver funeral spilling in the street
pass the street my father lived as a child
pass the house my aunt lived
pass the high school, that to tell a family secret
        my father was expelled from for inciting a race riot
pass the church I was baptized in, to pass an odd fact
                I've been baptized as many
   times as I've suffered a concussion
                      the number three
(lutheran, catholic church of god
or two car accidents, a work accident

one of which almost cost me an ear)
pass the street I live on longest
                suddenly, I can't tally all my haunted
  houses

everything passes in a few short miles
a small world, tiny histories, no one notices
except maybe this generation
                the one after, the one before

last call

ohio is forever
variable roadways eat speed
    it's the perfect night for speed
    the perfect night for adderall
    the perfect night for ephedrine
            but I never could handle speed
It makes my heart into a hummingbird dying
I already see things too clearly, too loud
speed makes all that vision hurt
instead, I eat miniature candy bars, altoids
chase a sugar rush, crash and repeat

tonight, orion's belt is guide
if unbuckled the sky
would rain corn stalks and bibles

corn stalks and bibles
it's twenty years ago
racing interstates after a sixteen-hour work day
crazy mike and a bag of doritos as passengers
frozen solid ohio
the night proves
all highways have ghosts
it's only a matter of how tired you are
            how split open you are

hit dayton five am
our buddy brian said we're twelve hours late
payphone calls, convenience stores, below zero nights
he's at his girl's place
he shook his roommate with telephones
his addled roommate who tried to kill himself a month
   before
stands at dorm entrance late night disheveled
holding open doors so we could crash
kill some sleep
nervous paranoid sleep

we skated around dayton less than twelve hours
parting with a snowstorm
on the other side of that front
I found my grandfather had a heart attack
I drove another three hours
caught and re-caught a storm
crashed the floor of an imaginary trailer park
dead
rattled nights
all these years
dead

my grandfather was gone in months
brian tossed a bullet in his head in '02
a failing marriage and no job were too much
unless you believe
his wife's parents knocked him off
to avoid a messy divorce

crazy mike blurted out brian's suicide to me
christmas eve
I was busy holding down a record shop
he was stalling, waiting, finally blurting
I excused myself to catch a cigarette
indianapolis seemed so far away

crazy mike is still crazy
we haven't talked much since the night
he clocked me in the face with a guitar
he chases demons that have already gotten away
last time we spoke he used words like schizophrenia

it's no surprise time escapes
rattles, drifts, evaporates
a nauseous dizzy feeling creeps
I wind engine up near a hundred
bleary, I should pull over
I'm too deep in my head
I can't stop

barely notice the deer
drop off accelerator, swerve, miss
expect a red and blue splash in the rearview
the officer, one a.m aviators
son, what's your hurry?
my eyes dilated diamonds
smile wide as stars says
baby, I'm just trying
to make pittsburgh for last call

only love can break your heart

when you're young and on your own
drunk, howling deep in the maryland night
trying to get the poison out of the soul
while poisoning the body

four am everything is alive
the alcohol kicked in
you want this to last and last and last
instead, kick a few hours' sleep
before hangover sun makes its move
then richmond, fucking richmond
you sick southern belle
always waiting for me
to make a bloodshot fool of myself

truck stop speed, hair of the dog
makes everything right
then blues in the maryland night
she shines through small crowds
red hair, blue eyes follow
your hands as they strum
d minor to a seven following
the g around to the chorus

after a few songs
she waits in your coat
you follow her to her dorm
she wishes you were there all the time

a college girl's statement to college boys
it's clear you're being placated

it doesn't change ceremony
the struggle to wring beauty from night
our ghosts, dream lovers
who turn to stars
to arrows in clasped hands
if you don't find what you want
at least you get what you need

she asks as the sun
comes apparent
would you like to get high?
slides from bed into panties
moves to the desk
meticulous with makings
sparks
returns
crawls into my chest

smoke hits lungs
I see the tragedy of her future
run across her eyes
I see every mile
annapolis to philly
run through my head
thin snow crust
makes tracks
covers tracks
I never need to be tethered
to any place again

the bird songs tonight

after a reading, crowd thins
cleveland poets back to cleveland
pittsburgh poets back under their rocks
one straggler looks for a couch
didn't make the usual twenty-four-hour reservation
I offer mine

silsbe and I talked after-party
I offer after-party even though
this poet doesn't seem like the late night
howling type
still he comes along
maybe we're rowdier than usual
the beer tastes great tonight
everyone is holding
the pipe is never not packed
always making the rounds
dude isn't participating
he turns green, sips his beer
uptight, brother needs a xanax bad
obvious if offered, he wouldn't partake

walking back to my place
late march and three am and beautiful
streets light aquarium glow
one lonely bird
sings a song
no birds sing on penn avenue
not at three am, or ever

my slow atom head
has interpreted this as a mating song

I interview every tree
looking for the bird
I want to have a long heart to heart
about loneliness
I want to remind the bird
no one is getting laid tonight
I can't find the bird
I stand in a parking lot
calling out
the bird needs to know
tomorrow will be better

I suppose I hadn't noticed
the poet dropped behind me
every sentence I utter
he says over and over
panic mantra
you're insane!

I unlock the door
he races upstairs
covers his head in a blanket
a knock-kneed ghost
scared of his own shadow

it's too late for admissions
I stand in the door
one word between my teeth
maybe

hold on cool breeze

penn avenue thursday nights
spring lets the breeze free
it blew me from lou's back porch
to sit under gallery lights: modern formations
words of poets change colors as they hit the air

return to the night
belt full of beer
lights spin color wheels
the moment the breeze kicks again
I lose my voice
stand frozen
with the last of winter
with the first of spring
with every cell of myself decimated
into tiny atom ghosts
neither ancient
or modern

I think about a friend
who wrote a song
full of jaunty melancholy
hold on cool breeze
I hear it turn the corner
rush through my head

when the feeling is gone
the night won't last so long
keep your eyes peeled for the light
the cool breeze gonna come and make it all right

manny theiner nods his head
as I pass, he's doing star wars raps
to impress kids half his age
they giggle, tug on 40's
silly islands they play in the street

a dude thuggin' it
leans into a garbage can
blunt cherries blow smoke halos
into the consciousness
of spak brothers flood light

I listen while I walk home
listen to the space in between seasons
where it seems years can pass

this night
walks with avenue saints
I find my footsteps
too familiar to notice darkness
to remember this street
they keep going
falling asleep
forever
in the passing
of each car's
taillights

take a break

a moustache
            drags a dead deer
                        into take a break bar

  orders a beer

        bellows

    I know a guy who will gut and clean it for you too!

some summers drop like flies

horizon
center wide
she picks music

I ask
the long way home?

she replies
the beautiful way
slithers around my arm
drops her head on my shoulder
from the corner of my eye
her smile

straight ahead
the way I don't know
sunset at peak

summer's birth
rests on her breath
as she sighs

tell me why

on the waves of the night
air so clear, it strangles
what's left of your thoughts

with tall trees
bugs pass time
buzz ears
it's possible the world ended
who could want anything more
than to get high?

there was a girl I knew
lived over garfield hill
she'd call late night
when alcohol reminded her
she was lonely

she was lonely
the end spiral of a divorce
those hard places
trying to make arrangements with yourself
that brackish waters deep in mind
where there's a need to flesh out
where he ended
where she began

there are a thousand ways to kill a night
to find ways to make darkness tolerable
to sift what's needed from what's wanted

in the end
we're only broken harbors
dreams and loneliness
to keep us afloat

dreams
burn out
on the way she smiles

loneliness
is the only thing
in life that compounds

better luck next year

(for todd tomasic)

the last pirate home game
the weather washes out
this season was a disappointment
but the temptation
of one last game is too much

nova's fastball is on
but it's the last game
players swing at anything

I fucking hate cubs fans
can't stand the rain
todd and I wait an hour into delay
five innings would be official
we start for the car
he's ahead in the warhol parking lot
wheelchair casters toss
rainbow lights around the overpass

through north side we talk urban renewal
how it cut the heart out of this neighborhood
on brighton, riggs glows, our fathers were regulars
my father a construction supply salesman
like his father before
todd's father a tin hammer
our fathers did the same job all their lives

serge chaloff's horn
all benzedrine heroin
bleats outside todd's apartment

I put together his chair
help him to the building
I say there's always next year
he says *next year will be better*
instead of amen, I say hopefully
we pause, consider silence

todd rolls up the ramp
over his shoulder
better luck next year

here's to your ex-wife

this bar smells like the color pink dying
I swear to never come back
even as I let that fog of smoke
that fucking smell
try to choke me out again

your ex-wife smiles at me
I give her a hug, we chat
before I head to the bar for a drink

I suddenly fail to recognize
the birthday girl
the mutants
or the guy who knows me
but I don't remember him

I'm admonished for allowing radio shows to die
for not having a funeral to mark
fifteen years of being a voice
I 'm told it's egoless to let things go sans ceremony
but sometimes it's simple
when a word falls off your tongue
it never needs to be spoken again

I orbit friends' conversations
monitor beer and time
eventually, I spiral to your ex-wife
she seemed ok with the divorce

tonight, it's the holidays
the regular weight of life
it's all too much

we never hit small talk
it's all her abyss
where three years went
how three years don't feel like they belong to anyone

I'm nearly forty
barely housebroken
with no idea how to console her
I remind her that she is free

I head back to the mutants
we talk shows we played
nights we spiked audience with mushroom
induced sounds, making rooms sparkle and slow

they're drunk and need a baritone
to anchor the jukebox
we sing billy joel
we sing the foundations

I see your ex-wife
across the bar
her face is a mask
building itself up
to fall apart

fuck you jay gatsby

a squall to stop midnight strong hearts
although the fury is barely an inch
out of the bar, snow globe streetlights
I offer her a ride, she has to go to her car

her car, where she lives now
although she sleeps with a man
she thought had *something* with
now it's a bed when there's nowhere
tonight, there is nowhere
tonight, there is snow

we glide downhill, laughing our asses off
                    times is hard
hell, we've been laughing for years
ever since regent square apartments
up till four, laughing and drinking
shit, times never get any better
anywhere or sciota street

she grabs two sweaters
boots, then abandons boots
alcohol braces wind chill
hard to believe its december
hard to believe a life fits in a trunk
hard to believe a college degree
ain't getting anyone anywhere

it's paper, there's no money in it
there's no money in anything
we scrape our change to laugh
gatsby's abandoned children
lost in america
the beautiful nowhere

she said if it was summer now
and she took her last final
she would drive until the car died
called wherever home

I think on north carolina afternoons
waiting storms out in pizza shops
talking about how the dead never come back
how it never gets easier to whistle with cotton mouth

we slide uphill, last buses whine
electronic voices canned stops
u-turns, wipers push snow
the road a tenuous ice world

south pacific
she gets out
snow will swallow her

as the door creaks
in the wind through vents
I'm sure I hear a rasp
fuck you, jay gatsby!

the ballad of dylan and jake

outside fort garland air is dust
I talk to blanca peak over an hour
but conversation with a mountain is tricky
I pass a trading post, see a couple
crust punks in black
bandanas up thumbs out

I drive past
I don't pick up hitchhikers
but no one should stand in a dust storm
on a one-hundred-degree day

jake, jumps in front
dylan, she's in back
happy for the ride
dylan has little to say
after five miles she's asleep

they met in a montana squat eight weeks ago
she's new orleans, he's mantua springs
they fell in love. caught a train south
tried to find new mexico, arizona
found they weren't welcomed

alex chilton's *flies on sherbet* plays
he's never heard big star
I tell him about the trip
he asks me about the east
curious about georgia

I tell him hot and green
he's not familiar with green
at least not east coast green

he's headed home
an easy two-hour ride
he's not excited for homecoming

he cracks confessional
the way only strangers can be
he found out his ex-girl
from home is pregnant
he's not sure it's his
but he has to go home
deal with it
deal with his
and her pissed moms

he's not sure what dylan's going to do
there ain't no place for her
in the dust storm of accidental creation

she's free to go, he doesn't want her to
she may go back to new orleans
a friend of hers was murdered recently
she wakes up nights saying her name
her friend is calling her home

I drop them with exit ramp in sight
a wanderer, a hanged man, a sleeping girl
the colorado evening to swallow us

it was a town called yukon

it was a town called yukon that led me astray
trashy coal camp hamlet with a one-way street
                half a stop sign
I miscounted lefts, complete a circle

at the beginning again
a chain restaurant dropped
roadside, suddenly I'm hungry

the last time I ate here was a year ago
after a shit reading for twenty dollars
in a deserted bend in the river town
the woman with me had finalized a divorce
now she has cancer

the waitress' name must be honey
all the businessmen call her that
they gawk at too much make-up, no ass and push up bra
                she asks if I'd like a drink
I swear it's the first words anyone ever said to me

air conditioning made me believe
a shandy was a good idea
it wasn't. a headache
crawls in with the sweetness

another businessman calls honey
all my crushes are on barmaids
      baristas and waitresses
women who talk to me
on days I've fallen off the map
today, I've fallen off the map

three boxers sit at the corner
I listen, half watch soccer
      nurse my shandy
they talk christian girls, diets and hangovers
      I can't take anymore

I call honey
ask for a to go cup
surprised she hands me one
I pour the remnants in

I'll nurse the too sweet taste
      another forty miles
when the beer gets too warm
I'll stop on a hill on a red dog road
where a dead black snake stretches
nine feet across
      the hit blew the skull
clear of the head. I lean over
pour the dregs on the corpse
      stare sun blind at nowhere
wait on resurrection that never comes

hagerstown sometimes

sometimes miles don't add to much
sometimes towns blend into a zen drone of non-distinctive
   road/traffic/landscape
sometimes there's only one diner left in town
sometimes that diner smells like a motel swimming pool
sometimes the waitresses bet on how long it will take you
   to leave
sometimes you hear them talking: how their feet hurt.
   how it's a goddamn miracle. how they appreciate each
   other. how they're fucking overwhelmed
sometimes you wander across the dead eyes of the
   patrons, wonder how they mark time
sometimes you order a crab cake sandwich while
   measuring your proximity to an ocean
sometimes after it's served you unfold a massive sheet of
   romaine, peel the rot
sometimes the waitress notices; *gee, they really gave you a
   tree, would you rather iceberg?*
sometimes you don't know if you should laugh at a
   suggestion
sometimes you think about the convenience store cashier
   who told you, it's a really good job, but she's tired. she'll be
   okay, she's done in an hour
sometimes the last four songs of *sticky fingers* knife
   through mountain roads as daylight burns
sometimes willie mays
sometimes you watch sunset through a big bay window,
   dusty light across vacant tables
sometimes in hagerstown, you wonder if the sun hasn't
   already set

redneck's paradise

across the west virginia line
she reaches into her purse
pulls a jim beam pint
helps herself
leans over
kisses me
offers the bottle

sometimes all you have left is to celebrate your escape

like neil young in *albuquerque*

the couple at the door
see my shirt
ask if I brought the rain
if I knew them better, I'd say
in this town the rain has a habit of following you
it's a thing you can't shake
solitary, dark clouds, at your heels
endlessly

today I feel like neil young in *albuquerque*
wanting breakfast, a joint and anonymity
I've felt this way for several seasons
clawing and uncomfortable
something I can't shake
so instead, I ease into it
half measures

the waitress yawns, waits for order up
I used to come here with my grandfather
weekly dinners in the wake of my father's death
his best attempts to be part of my life
never knowing how to relate

I think of my father who if you asked him
what he wanted for breakfast he always said
eggs benedict. I never saw him order it
strange even at the far end of our cities
we still find our histories glaring

while eating eggs benedict, I wonder
if turning forty has everything to do with this feeling
age puts weight on you, I mean that metaphorically
I consider my father dead over thirty years
my grandfather gone over twenty
I consider generations
all the boughs of a bloodline tree

red shirted cooks
spin around an open range
an array of belgian waffles and strawberries, of eggs
    and toast
of home fries a la carte, of greek omelets appear
out of the tornado, the ballet, the flickers of fire
this furnace glows indelible, forever

a young black kid and an old marine bus
when they pause, I see the same look on their faces
the indignity of work, the pain of physical labor
is it a muscle memory or generational memory?
our dreams, squeezed out of us doing so much for nothing

the rain mostly stopped
couples cringe under their umbrellas
I cross *the bridge to take when things get serious*
I turn around at the north versailles welcome sign
then cross it again

edgar thompson works looks the same
as the cover of jack gilberts *tough heaven*
his poems flash, one line surfaces
we find the heart by dismantling what the heart knows

the great american apple pie fight

I found snow white
seven dwarfs
spiderman
laurel and hardy
the blues brothers
dancing
while holding still
outside the
petersburg chamber of commerce
while
lee greenwood
sang the chorus
of
proud to be an american
an endless loop
...
I was moved
...
I was moved
...
it was like
I had an apple pie fight
with god

tony brush park has sinks and restrooms
(for fredrico fellini)

silsbe turns his car into an accordion
to fit the last free spot in fairview
1-2-3 street,
american flags, italian flags
sewn together
italian american
never forget

early for a reading
with adventure in our hearts
east cleveland without a map
j & l fest, the feast of the assumption
the virgin mary never dies
she rides cloud cars to heaven
I don't believe in heaven
what if instead of dying
we all got to ride cloud cars

this is little italy proper
a street fair crammed into five blocks
sublime is playing
I don't feel italian
I feel thirsty

la dolce vita
collins and silsbe order beer

I order stella artois
if it's good enough for slayer
it's good enough for me

stella is awful
but it's too hot for boozy beers
wipe the foam mustache away
I swear I catch a glimpse of
marcello mastroianni

I swear he was buzzing toward the patio
sneaking past the pavarotti/ sutherland poster
ahh marcello, beware false idols

outside I see him in the alley
with the other old men
leering at teenage girls
in summer short shorts
placing bets
which ones
in back seats
in back yards
under hazy strings of light
will lose their virginity tonight

then as the priest
goth monotone through
church steps service
was that the nicene creed?
was it the prayer of the eucharist?

through him with and in him
in the unity of the holy spirit
all glory and honor is yours
almighty father
forever and everrrrrrrrrr

we need another bar
we need a patio
more cold beer
this is happening

people jam the streets
everyone who is working
everyone who is drinking
a pug ties a cherry stem with its tongue

I don't know if I want to read poems
tonight
anymore
I want to stay
in this strange catholic world
unstuck in time

I saw a room for rent
1929 1-2-3 street
the landlords name
maria carletti
almost eighty
broken english
morning and evening church

a novena at two pm everyday
she believes no women in the rooms
she believes lights out at eleven

I sign the lease
with lemon juice
and powdered sugar
ahh maria, beware false idols

silbe and collins take off
wedding present blares
as accordion returns to corolla

I am free here
disco inferno on the street stage
six tickets for a hot sausage sandwich
five more for a ride on the ferris wheel

I wander down euclid avenue
to lake view cemetery
the city crawls
the university
the hospital
try to destroy east cleveland

time rides a cloud car
the sky is a symphony
the embouchure of heat lightning
the skyline foxy in the dusk

I drink bad beer
and give my heart to you
east cleveland

I pray rain heals stigmata
I pray for rain
nothing gentle
I want biblical rain
I want all of lake erie
dumped on my lap
I want clouds to remind me
jb, beware of false idols

pavey at the waffle house

(for shawn pavey)

last night of tour
somewhere outside
blue springs missouri
in a waffle house parking lot
cops bust a driver nearby
red and blue lights swirl

we're alive in strange madness tonight
we've been listening to words for days
           digging for the next batch of stories
we're tired and words are rebelling

in a circle new friends prepare goodbyes
each of us are the stars and the moon
pavey, paid for our feast
he has one more poem to recite
from memory, my memory doesn't recall
what was perfect in his verse
what seemed like it summed
this moment succinctly, crystalline
in the weight of the fall night
somehow everything we see
everything we believe
is even more beautiful
when we know it's escaped

al's bar

one am
drunk
corner
of
sixth
and
north limestone
hoping
each
street
light
is
the
moon

dial s for sonny

I: sonny's crib

through the grease of midnight windows
the redwood inn hotter than a blast furnace
the piano player plays stride   boogie woogie blues
patrons sweat in swelter, shake their wicked knees. pelvis on
    pelvis grinding
misbehaving under dim bulbs, a week's work wearing out
forgetting itself in gyrations and groping
all those frustrations goin' down in the ministration of
    cheap liquor
the smile on the piano player's face shines. pint of gin wobbles
    on the piano
a half full jar full of dimes shakes, rings, sounds of sleigh bells

they see you out there sonny, wide eyed, waiting on the devil
they know you from around, nowhere to escape in a coal camp
this sister town, a sister to a mine shaft, scattered immigrants
crammed in company duplexes speaking scattered languages
at foreman and bosses, at a system that keeps them scattered

these folks know you, your family living in rooms above the
    dance hall
mother, brothers and sisters quartered together
these people know you, the mischief of children too young
    for work
the women see your games of tag as they drag victrolas into
    the yard

drop needle, swing robust hips, hang laundry on the line
everyone here knows you bang on the piano every
    chance you get
they know your fingers as they hit ivory. they've heard
    you practice
heard you in church race across keys nimble through
    spirituals full of pain
your fingers chase sounds from beautiful women's lungs
then fall behind as the reverend's basso profundo blares

tonight, they remember your fingers. white, black,
    poor miners, they want to hear them play
they invite you, coo at you, the piano player coaxes
    from his seat
the music calls you, we're waiting on the devil
no gin for a boy. piano player puts you on his lap you
    put hands over his
he plays a couple like that, like that, you got it boy,
    you got it!
hands possessed, fingers blister humid yellow keys
cigarette smoke, building shakes, praise from a
    degenerate congregation
ooh's and ahh's
that's right baby, that's right!
yelps possessed   held in sway   they're in your hands
    now little man
you know this is all you want from now on

you stumble upstairs exhausted, six am, mamma's
    gonna tan your hide

maybe she even tries but when she grabs you, pockets
    jingle, stuffed with dimes
you fish handfuls, penance angry breaks to smiles
your daddy died weeks after you were born, black lung
    made sure thing never were right
but things are always gonna be tight ain't no changing it

you know you can play your way out
all the dances, in church, on the radio, every chance
you're gonna hustle, hustle down dirt roads from herminie
down dirt roads from irwin   down dirt roads to pittsburgh
through nights of a thousand stars, forever in wylie avenue
    smoke
its bars electric alive!
bop is born!

the past escapes afternoon grey
I read the landscape of wendell road
flick pictures I've memorized, place you where I can
on the berm, stare at a vacant lot where the redwood
    burned seventy years ago
up the hill, a line of houses, this is where you were born,
    where you lived
this lot choked by stinging nettle, knotweed chutes, plastic
    bags and deer shit
blue minor plays through car window, I lean against the door
wait for vision, wait for time to converge, stare through place
to try to get these ghosts to jump out from the past and dance

II: leapin' and lopin'

sonny leads the band to the head
the steelers lost the game   maybe the season
pajich and amy, silsbe and I sit in christmas light shine
we smoke dope out of a quarter inch socket
change color, tell stories
leapin' and lopin'
voodoo

horns call the theme, wander variations, cracked back
    on the down beat; billy higgins accent
I give bob shit for taping a quarter to his tone arm to
    get records to play through
he has an old 50's console system more furniture than
    turntable, all wires loose
touch the treble, bass goes up
touch the volume, you get treble

charlie rouse takes first solo, trips at the end of his
    phrase, winds a mistake in
we're entranced. butch warren's two note background
    holds it down. it's not hard to play
but you gotta have touch, you gotta have touch, just
    the slightest   touch

bob can't understand why this song isn't famous it has
    a henry mancini compositional cool
that should have had white audiences begging
    it should have been a hit

but with way more soul, some eternal spirit, some danger
some deep blood, some haunted dread
that deep weathered sonny clark sadness
heroin or loss? Is it the bad dreams that come as your artist
heart pinned to your sleeve bleeds across keys?

turrentine's trumpet breaks clear blue reaches staccato
bob almost lost all his records in wilkinsburg one night
he forgot them on his roof, didn't notice them missing
until he crossed *the bridge to take when things get serious*
he turned around, found them strewn across the road
no one hit them, no one touched them
I look at the cover see a pavement scrape

sonny clears space, all finesse, keys coaxing blues in note
    flurries
higgins works wood block
we are stoned lost
lost in tone
    lost in a geography of grooves
                witchcraft out of seventy year old speakers

we geek out, favorite players, born from this, sparked by this
I'm riding high, the other night my ears touched a second
    press
john coltrane's blue train, sonny plays on it
pretty, heavy vinyl, deep black, petrol slick after sixty years
dead wax playlite ear winks
when needle touches groove, the sound so clear it stops my
    heart

    bababaBa bomm bomp
                      bababaBa bomm bomp

turrentine, rouse call everyone back to the theme
    restated softer
softer   softer   till speaker's hush
otis redding the cat wanders in, bumps legs a shark
    stalking affection
I think of a lost afternoon, lake mendota, madison
    wisconsin holding summer green
I careened highway loops searching for monuments
memorials to a plane crash
that killed this cat's namesake

III: dial s for sonny

first of december unseasonably warm mist slips to
    rain off and on
I have time to kill. I remember an article stating sonny
    clark is buried
st mary's, sharpsburg, then the pic of the tree line near
    the grave
I stand damp, read geography for familiar places in my
dusty brain

I spent an evening here fifteen years ago with a girl,
    a star chart
we tried to pick out: cassiopia, ursa, orion
I can barely find one of those constellations
we paid more attention to each other than the stars that night

I think of that *paris review* article
harrowing moments clark and lyn halliday at w eugene
    smith's place
smith in the other room develops photo's, halliday cooks,
    sonny ties off
plunger starts down
sonny slips away
groans and gurgles
drool dribbles down his chin
halliday panics
the night his girlfriend brought sonny around with cpr
    still clear
sonny fades, halliday shouts
Sonny Can You Hear Me!
Sonny Can You Hear Me!
skin on skin slaps sonny's face
Sonny Stay With Me!
Sonny
SONNY
SONNY!

no one knows where you go, there's a galaxy only right here
floating the bliss warm never. parallel as now. flat reality
    blossoms
the interdimensional fog winds a sheet across the body
we're all waiting on the devil
sonny slowly slides back   revived   resurrection
pressure loaded into his body, life sparks across a
    spinal column, lightning centers the brain
haliday never mentions it, sonny washes sweat off his face

sonny fixes himself, rolls down his sleeve
they both split for a cheeseburger

at the hill crest
once a season you see the allegheny
now there's only bridges, cars move here to nowhere
the long defunct henry miller steel spring factory sparks
    the sky
its workers' shadows hang on clouds

I walk back to the car and catalog an inventory of names
germans and poles, serbs and italians, greeks and scotch
    irish
buried on this hill, maybe with family, maybe alone
all resting under granite, under iron bar crosses under lead
    pipes with concrete nubs
under ground
where you can't tell any
of their bones
apart

obvious now, I remembered the wrong cemetery
there's another graveyard on the other hill
I become clouds, move with the afternoon
greenwood cemetery almost forgotten
you easily define the difference between the black and
    white sections
even in death the system segregates
in minutes I match the photo in my head
In this section headstones are scarce

the dates that exist match 1963
no one placed a stone, everything is approximate
I stand withered in weather, sick to my stomach

sessions dried up in 62
ike quebec, dexter gordon, grant green
you were all dried up, a shell until you sat at the piano
no surprise the last overdose came
needle in the arm forgotten harlem shooting gallery
the guy you shot up with dead too
cops didn't give a fuck, wrapped you both
in body bags not caring which dead junkie was which
hell, you may be in a long island potter's field
no matter who is buried here
the baroness koenigswarter
patron and refuge of the era of jazz
paid for your flight home

in sharpsburg I watch old women carry groceries
up sharps hill, as it's been for 200 years
I count wood houses regularly washed in river

I listen to *it ain't necessarily so*
gershwin as rave-up hip sixties soul style
grant green as leader, tears across the strings
sonny solos fire
they both lock something beautiful
        something spiritual
                something beyond
art blakey's thunder sticks rattle foundations

he hollers through solos
hollers as they trade licks
he was witness!
he saw the light!
motherfucker, we hope to be this beautiful!

riggs' lounge

all it takes is a quarter
flipped or tossed
from anywhere in the bar
into the tall clear beer stein
to the left of the register
to open the doors
of heaven

between cedarville and pearl

he thumbs pocket new testament
fumbles revelations
bag of shit chinese food
between his legs
cigarette between fingers
waits on dusk
the bus
neither come anytime soon

109 n. graham

I hit my head on the second moon
pass along the moon's greeting

pajich, kukulski
speak
sing
mumble
gross high school dance harmony
out of key
crescendo
caterwaul
as the juke
coughs
sam cooke's
cupid

9 stories

samoan cats
cover
how's the cat
I can't keep from crying

goddamn
I shouldn't have
worn this shirt
tonight

beechwood farms

tiny waterfall
blackbird calls
silence
to any thought
that clutters
my head

evening watch

mama bald eagle
runs distraction

her young call
across the river

six miles into
a nine mile hike

cobwebs in my beard
flies form halos

mescaline

    I was looking
for the true image of god

    all I found
my face   reflected
    in toilet water
    as I vomited

reasons to hate being poor

the bar bathroom
an inch of piss on the floor
holes in both of my shoes

susquehanna river blues

how many times
across the
susquehanna
to get
nowhere

fric and frac

I slam six tacos
while the only
female body builder
in westport
gives advice
on spray tans

39th street blues

dog shit
miller lite coaster
salon beyond

union hill prayer

the sun
and the city skyline
as main street crests
at union hill

sonny clark's piano
silences
the silver bullet
calivan

this is our church

mizzou

the cashier talks tattoos
the couple ahead
buy
two hot dogs
a sixer of bud lite lime

the woman grabs his ass
he pays with a hundred

indiana billboard (found poem)

service as
warm as
our biscuits

new year's day

to wake up
certain
nothing's
changed

for the beloved dead of delaware

that nearly full moon
those stars
the clouds
wave over the sky
       over the ocean

I got lost frozen
my mind grabs this image
transposes it to van gogh
starry night over the rhone

vincent, in your paintings
I see every atom, every vibration
all the spaces between matter
in the coarse simplicity of a brush stroke

you saw too much of the world
I see too much of the world
tonight, all this useless beauty
is too goddamn much

I park myself in a bar
wring all the noise out of the world
a tolerable level to sleep
a tolerable change in the weather

I greet the sunrise anticlimactic
on the dunes a woman says
the clouds won this one

today north and west roads
will take me home
I don't know what order
I pick at random

today silhouettes of black birds
drain from each passing tree

today raptors police the sky

today every church
is one room full
quaint steeple
to reach the sky

I wanna stop
I wanna look in
listen to flat note hymns
I wanna hear a homily
wrap the new year in jesus

the cemeteries are frozen
still in the same way they were consecrated
proof all we leave the world with
is a stone and a handful of bones

cielito lindo

(for jose faus)

jose talks about a beach in mexico
between christmas and new year's it's virtually empty
except for villagers from the mountains who
live in shanties and fish. there's a few tourists
mostly germans, a few americans

bonfires and shacks burn on new year's
the germans sing *o tannenbaum* as a chorus
the mexicans sing *cielito lindo* as a chorus
the americans shuffle and look at their feet
no song or celebration in their hearts

the beach is known for turtles
who lay their eggs then head back to the sea
when their young hatch they head for the sea
thousands of tiny turtles crawl slowly to the sea

we're in cleveland jose
after reading in RA's house with all its energy
we walk state road through the ukrainian village
a russian and polish village nearby
beautiful gold leaf domes rise to glow
in city darkness. icons celebrate
ceremonies we don't understand
of course we understand, we're human

no bar is open on sunday night
you, me and silsbe
we trail after neon, parched
crawl back to george avenue like turtles
wait on strong drink herbal refreshments and burroughs
our stories celebrate life, improbability
we loiter around the calivan
the eyes of leda upon us
we hope the neighbors won't care
enough to call the cops

for anna karina

...

she's a cartoon, she twirls a six shooter in powder burned
hands that rifle through dead man's pockets finding only
toothbrush/paste, they share similar legacies

..

she sings as tears go by as suburban typewriter
realizes sentences are useless, the floor stubbed out a
cigarette, this is why marlon brando looks desperate

...

she's the devil that occupies second rate lonely tragedies
the right to remain silent, she loads a gun, a parrot reads
a newspaper, the telephone waits on a gunfight. there is
no mystery, the south pole ran off with a bartender

...

she's the color of time, forever elsewhere in the mirror
a window not much older than rock and roll
clear, without desire. she's a war that's never over

...

she's a cross country audience, a sailboat, a miniskirt
so cruel, so obsolete, her real name a mystery
of handcuffed influence

...

she's a dress drenched in blood, disturbed silence
she turns beautiful to smoke, she marks time occasionally
exquisite as jack ruby

...

winner, winner chicken dinner

(for john dorsey)

I watch paternity court
in the rialto, wait out the afternoon
there's a girl four or five
she hides among the barstools
she jumps out occasionally, yells
BOO!

I'm sure not much has changed
since you read at the teatro
there are still underage ghosts
hoping to be served
pittsburgh street still runs east west
cosmic bowling still brings them out
when they get old enough
they graduate to the headkeeper

you said this is a drifter's town
the furthest isosceles angle
of pennsylvania's own bermuda triangle
it seems everything here disappears

I haven't heard a bigfoot call
as I wade in post-industrial debris
watch the beaten faces
barely flicker with emotion

the only building drawing a crowd
is the behavioral health center

you know john, lately I feel
like I'm being haunted by van gogh
today, I may be lost in the potato eaters

the woman who waited on me
blood vessels burst behind her right eye
she tells someone she's old
and tired and had enough

it's your birthday, babe
nowadays each plume of smoke
is twenty years
is forty years

somehow time flows
until it's time to kick out
the crypt doors
screaming

it's time to bleed out another year
squeeze everything out of twilight
it's all coming brother
it's all light speed

unconditional surrender

somethin' 'bout mississippi makes you lonely
same could be said for anywhere
summer twilight in the hill country
cicadas, bats, roaches, frogs, crickets
hum massive unison, a sound experience
dizzy on the shore, clouds trace in the dark

morning sun warms lake
warms surrounding woods
dragonflies and mosquitos take over
the sun, the warm bring out
summer smells, magnolia and yellow pine
I swear I smell her next to me
I think about that last night in west virginia

she was recovering
an abusive husband
a miscarriage
divorce yet to be filed
we were having fun
it didn't get serious 'til I hit the road
absence and the heart
a month of phone sex
in motel parking lots
cell phone moonlit windshields
can you call that love?

on returning, not ready to join the world
we spent the weekend, her apartment
champagne and pot brownies
scrabble for recovery, before returns to couch
or bedroom to cover promises
whispered from the far-flung fiber optic dark

then west virginia, every sentence an argument
she scratched with questions
reaching for something deeper
children and marriage, husbands and wives
she walks around indirectly
I answer accurately
I knew we were done when she told me she prayed for me

vicksburg motel walls talk
transient voices casualty and alcohol
drop my bag, look at both beds
I miss the hell outta her sometimes
I can't figure why
almost wish I had service, I'd call her
if only to hear the phone turn to ice

in a gift shop I buy postcards
one of u.s grant handsome in a chair
uniform coat open, cigar, muddy riding boots
the back says they called him unconditional surrender

beaumont texas, I slept like shit last night
javelina in the bush root and dance
haggard mornings, the contractions
the expansions of the road move quickly
when the brain has only a horizon to consider

in a diner I stare at postcards, rest on grant
I write her address, not her name
in the subject field
maybe?
no stamps, I leave it
on the table with the tip

payphone hymnals

I found the last working payphone
outside a gas station
near chillicothe ohio
I stood in the booth a minute
phonebook gone, push buttons
coin slots scarred it smelled
like time stopped
I thought about calling
even though I don't remember
the last time we spoke
I wanted to remind you
of that night I called
from a payphone
outside an abandoned donut
shop in the parking lot
of a motel in memphis
I gave you my room phone
as cops rolled in five deep
lights flashing, I may have
used the drug phone
I slid back to my room
waited on your call
I answered, stretched
the cord to the window
stared through curtain cracks
watched the cops
drag a man with a bleeding head

in cuffs and boxers out
of the room next to me
I didn't tell you what was
happening, you were lonely
I wanted you to believe
I was and everything was safe

4113 bethoven (christ on the cross)

across walk boards to the slop sink
the guy digging out the sewer line yells
watch out we found needles in there

I turn the water on, look in the other basin
candy bar wrappers, hangers, coffee cans
a pair of shorts, a burnt spoon, other debris

I look up, plastic christ on the cross
leans on the seam of the window

paul newman once said
nothing is a real cool hand

I look out the window
feel outside air blow cold
from an open dryer vent

the wound in white jesus' side
glows red, his head down
I can't see his eyes
to know if he's lost

jumbotron

we were a motley looking pair
justin's father had just died
he was suffering a break-up
he had long dyed black hair
a duster trench coat worn
all seasons and dog chains
when he took off his coat
he'd taken to cutting

I was five years under
waterlogged in heavy depression
not helped by working overnights
not sleeping, not eating, I was skeletal
one hundred twenty-five pounds
of wobbly flesh, swiveling through
a world that was too much

we were friends, lovers of baseball
sunday afternoon freaks out
in that freak show year
looking for a pale skinned overdose
of vitamin d and a barely 500 team
still clinging to playoff hope
somehow in august

that stadium was a monolith of concrete
an empty toilet bowl

in those darkest of years you were guaranteed
an entire section for a general admission ticket

climbing to our seat way up on the ring
beyond peanut heaven we're stopped
the fed-ex guy offers a free upgrade
general admission is magically
behind home plate
we are winning

to new seats
he hates picking couples
they run off before the fourth
when the winners are on the jumbotron
it's usually husbands stepping out
not wanting to get busted on the big screen
in front of fifteen thousand tumbleweeds
bleary eyed from the excitement of subpar baseball

fourth inning, we're announced
pomp and circumstance and a couple
of fucked up freaks on the jumbotron
waving to the sunday crowd

the sunday crowd
the whole stadium
gasps
you could hear children sob
as the camera operator cut away

solaris

(for andrei tarkovsky)

I sit, watch fall forever
watch leaves fall forever
one at a time, one at a time, one at a time

sometimes it rains
sometimes it rains
      forever
colloidal, viscous rain

I think in terms of video
how our mind films clouds
how there's always a horse
these expressions in images
the ocean, the influence of our thoughts

everything in our lives is anachronistic
our futures misremembered
to keep time in order
the past, a ladder
that swallows its own tail

a hive mind, we are connected to a hive mind
we feed its ocean with our thoughts
we build realities in banal nonsense
in imaginings of our selves
there is no big reveal

I found the edge of time
sitting on my tongue
I sat there and burned
the remnants of myself

they say that you always remember
your first look at space
I always remember looking at the ocean
I wonder if the ocean is happy
I wonder about the hive mind agitated by fear
I wonder if we get the same nervous tastes
      simultaneously
I wonder if we took a poll of fears
if we all weren't experiencing the same things
but we ran out of words
so we edited ourselves
   we edited time
cut in little nostalgic portraits
all the happy memories of being
humans, oceans, horses, hives

throw out your suicides
these generations see the end
but they never die. our time is built on
but can't stomach its own resurrection

we own the night

(for renee alberts)

I was in a wal-mart
in moundsville west virginia
when you texted
you went nuclear

hell, I've know you
fifteen years, always fierce
but I knew the life you chose
didn't sit with you

you texted tonight:
I'm leaving town
sorry I missed you till now
can we meet later?

a question sits on the bar
how can you love people
who don't love themselves?

we shoot bulleit
you walk me through
walking out of your life
that moment on a beach
staring off into the pacific
you realized you were living
someone else's life

that moment you realized
you didn't know why
was it what you were told you should want?
was it only for security?

I've had that moment many times
staring at the pacific, the atlantic
on the gulf of mexico, at sunrise
and sunset on lake champlain
almost twenty years apart
I've had that moment in so many places
it's a hard moment
these are difficult question
but questions to be proud of
    questions with no easy answers

we race time tonight
try to squeeze everything
into a last physical conversation
we talk about freedom
we talk about letting go
we talk about isolating
the noise that holds us in place
how in that isolation
it may be possible to find
what you actually need
we talk more about freedom

we own the night tonight
all its useless beauty

as sunday sleepers
fog through dreams
of their disaster lives

I drive you back to your folks
you're full of what it all means
I've never seen you
more confident
more beautiful
than when you walked away

zoloft

that night sticks out, clear
like nothing else in those months
I woke up with no voice, I mean
I had a voice, it was so far inside
I couldn't coax the motherfucker out
I sat on the couch
didn't and couldn't feel much
restlessness drove me out
streetlights had a strange glow
I stopped by work to find someone
instead I watched everyone leave
I felt like a panic attack, I'd never had a panic attack
couldn't understand why humans were green
I watched co-workers, friends pass
it was too much for my voice to jump out
I'm here, tell me everything's alright
I followed the cars out, hit the highway, drove half the night
no idea where, until I was home
then I slept for a month

my mother left my stepfather
my brother was recovering from a near fatal accident
my grandmother in poor health, needed constant care
I was alone with this, not equipped
with the tools to understand
a psychotic episode
a nervous breakdown
another salvo in an endless fight with depression

I spent years underwater
when I started working over night
I stopped sleeping, stopped eating
that didn't help

my mother and I stumbled
into a heated argument
the next day she said
I scheduled a doctor's appointment

the family doctor's first question
are you on drugs?
in an accusatory manner
you might say I lost it

he prescribed zoloft
told me sometimes we get sad
its ok to be sad
my head saying *fuck you*
this was more complicated than being sad

a month of free samples
life was brighter at the edges
I felt blood move in my head
the first time someone said something
my reaction was *alright cool*
when the reaction inside
fuck you asshole
that was the last time I took zoloft

back for a checkup
I said I flushed them
color went out of his face
he reminded me it's alright to be sad
it's alright to ask for help

icon

I see blue colors better than anyone
I see no awe, no faith left
only vanity   ashes
only the sin of pride

this faithless world
puts out its eyes when it sees beauty
    wisdom is ignorance
        sin comes through grief

eve in the garden
braids the hair of a dead horse

eve as the magdalene
naked in a fur coat
leaps a fire

get out of my sight serpent

my legs full of ants
I live your torment

give me a blanket
I'll become a bird

if it snows in summer
you may find me silent

you may say
he has sinned, he is atoning

I plead with the lord alone
christ was crucified out of love
and only in a dream

we have dreams
to be above the earth
liberated from the physical body

when the world has swallowed everyone
we will rise above sin and dirt
to see with god's eyes

postcard from belle missouri

I got a room that straddles the county line
a water tower overhead
pronounces the town name
for travelers coming north, south
on route twenty-eight

two beagles chase across yards
shrill barks at the wind

the boo radley house
at the corner of third
roof collapsed
into a wide-open grin

the sidewalk starts
at the catholic church
parishioners leave
imbued in sunday morning light

the baptist church
parishioners arrive
a multi-color truck
no muffler passes once
        passes twice
the driver waves

the garage door collapsed
on itself, boarded back up
plywood to fill the gaps

the fire plug beckons
from sometime in the sixties
the old oak tree
lords over a vacant corner lot
waves from another era

the screen door, house number
410, blows in the morning wind
the livestock auction barn
dominates
the corner of fourth and alvarado
the car wash stares back

the patrons in the café
down coffee, biscuits and gravy
the sign on the pool hall door
no weapons allowed in the pool hall

the bakery long since closed
the auto garage that caught fire
the carbon stained door
not opened in years

a woman smokes
bitches out a man
in camo and ball hat
she quiets, we pass
he makes eye contact
sheepishly nods

the glory hole

at the intersection
of a road to climax springs
and a road to hurricane deck
we spy the glory hole
next to tres hombres
near the pontoon graveyard

it's like where's waldo here
can you recognize every mention
of *glory hole*
as ceiling fans swirl smoke

two and a quarter gets
a bud light draft
frosted mug, twenty
an hour gets your
boat a designated driver

cigarettes burn in an ashtray
for the better part of millennium
one man overjoyed at being drunk
plays a dropkick murphys song
insists we all sing along
he pumps fists, prompt to the bar
as the chorus comes in

kiss me, I'm shitfaced!

oscar's diner

an elderly couple
creak out of a
sport utility vehicle
is this a good place to eat?

lost in the fifties
classic american diner
chrome plated style
the prettiest girl
in jefferson city
is hostess, she stops
teenage boys dead

the waitress
is a hummingbird
weighed down
by a four barrel
stainless steel
coin changer

she wears failure
smeared eyeshadow
and mashed potatoes
dorsey offers consolation

there is no wrong answer
when it comes
to a choice
of gravy

winter 1979

corner of bethoven and apollo
hanging drywall in a warehouse
no running water
piss in a bucket
scan the east side of the city

shake dry wall dust out my hair
the sun in this city
is the strange case of jekyll and hyde

when it's grey
with brutal winter light
it could still be hell with the lid off

when it's sunshine
especially in the spring
especially in the fall
I swear it's the garden of eden

today, as I look
at the immaculate heart of mary
it's both at the same time

pellegrino lived down the street
late 70's, he's telling stories
I can't keep dates straight
let's say winter 79

he climbed that douglas fir
drunk
cut twelve feet off the tree
so his wife could have
the christmas she wanted

he talks about chessie
a polish drunk
a few hairs over five feet
who stuttered
and played the accordion
he fired howitzers during the great war
his brain never recovered

his sister was in an institution
after his parents died
he couldn't afford it
so he moved her in with him
lived off her social security checks

she died near the end of the month
he didn't call the cops
didn't call the coroner
waited days till her next check came
bought a ton of beer
drank himself silly
then called the coroner
who couldn't tell when she died
her skin was wax
her ears were black

they covered her in a sheet
took her away
while chessie rambled
he fed her breakfast that morning

chessie claimed he married spanish ann
who no one ever saw
but when he mentioned her
he'd wheeze in nasal voice
blue spanish eyes
tears falling from your spanish eyes
it sounded nothing like humperdinck

alcohol got the better of chessie
he lost the house, taxes and loans
no more iron city pounders
he died alone
in one of those goddamn government rest homes

wilmerding

sparrows nests
hang on each letter
valley auto parts

the blue haven

sky opens
in summer squall
the blue haven
electric neon smothers outside eaves
hisses and hums
the soundtrack to backseat cocaine

smog veil opens
on a five dollar cover
outside sign
glitz this saturday

glitz is responsible
for the quiet riot cover
bartender says they used to be
9-1-1

bikers have no idea
why we're overdressed
ian paid the cover for the bride
and groom yet to arrive

seated, exhausted
how many drinks have I had
since the industrial hell mouth
gave birth to ceremony?
I can't remember

don't care
I drink myself
disappointed
sober

fingers loop in suspenders
bride and groom
take shots
I nurse workers' tears
sweet child o' mine
half step down
limps sans second guitar

someone is high school catching up
someone asks for a tampon
someone asks about the wedding
we pick the bones of a commemorative box of cookies
debate to even odds the next song
it's a struggle as it breaks the verse
shit, I hadn't heard trixter since 1990

tonight, our time machine falls off the table

hymn to garfield hill

there's pizza in the fridge
why don't we grab a slice

my roommate left for work
no reason to grab at garment scatter
it's too hot for clothes anyway

leaning against the counter
the rise above water tower
wears the first seconds of july sun

cool air from the fridge, cold pizza on the stove
two arms around one body
face buried in her hair
she laughs, chews mouth open
breaks and passes pieces over her shoulder

why don't we get back in bed
shake the birds out of
the trees one more time

let's let hymns bloom
in the sky over garfield hill
before sweat stings our eyes to sleep

the great pittsburgh pierogie race a'nat

it was a playoff game at the bloomfield bridge tavern
    the best place for a playoff game
it was pirates and cardinals
an empty bar, except a group of friends
I don't remember which game it was
honestly, I don't remember if they won
I'm sure it was paulie's idea

they're home we should have our own
    pierogie race a'nat
sheila took it seriously

pierogies arrive
butter and onion dreams
polish potato perfection

we personalize our pierogies
sharpies on toothpick polish flags
each pierogie an individual
like at the home games

cut to commercial
home half of the sixth
we each shot putt a pierogie
a derelict olympiad

the hallowed faithful
after twenty years of losing
send playoff dreams down
the bar covered in butter

whichever pierogie made it
farthest won, I remember
that winning pierogie
a snail trail of animal fat
glistening under dim lights
lying still alone on the bar

sometimes losers get lucky
sometimes there's just a little hope
      that makes it worthwhile to sit
                      to watch
                      to cheer

the night the fireflies taught dave brubeck to keep time

after a few rounds
she says, *let's take a walk in the cemetery*
better idea, I reply
let's go back to my place
roll a joint, THEN go for a walk in the cemetery
her eyes light, *perfect!*

it's past sunset
the pizza shop next door sells beer
wanna split a quart of beer?
how could anyone say no?

she's heard tales of foxes
I have seen foxes
usually at dusk, on still nights
you may hear the pups
yips and yelps, mingling
bat sirens, nighthawks, whitetail snorts

it's a perfect night to sit in the grass
light rain occasional
we're laughing too hard
telling too many stories
to tell if there's foxes
the alcohol, the joint
raise her voice

more manic than its usual
steady huskiness

I need a stenographer for these nights
the madness of my friends
all these accidental poets
letting their hair down
letting their hearts beat comfortable

we sit, lightning bugs
rise glow steady
¾ time
you swear tonight
is the same night
they taught brubeck
how to keep time

maybe a mantra

it doesn't look like august
the cemetery green
unsinged by summer heat
the rain keeps coming
leaves everything lush
it doesn't really get hot here anymore
it doesn't really get cold here anymore

the bank is closed
on butler street I almost
get t-boned by someone not
paying attention to traffic
even the refineries look like heaven
the 62nd street bridge, sharp's hill
lose themselves, time is the equivalent
of nothing, time is nostalgia dying

last night we had a wake
for a favorite bar, we talked
how many shows, how many dollar
skunked beers we've drank, we are
the age of things that aren't there anymore
we question our moorings, our anchors

I woke to news of hate rallies
disconcerted
you will not replace us

you will not replace us?
there is no permanence to this world
we only have a modicum of control
over the lives we lead, I'm sure that's
hard for people to admit, to exert
force to retain some fleeting control
is madness, an unhealthy sense
we mean more in the eye of the universe

everything we see here will someday be gone
everything we know will someday be gone
everyone, everything will be gone
I find comfort in that personally

I cross the allegheny again
follow the s curves up negley
toward home, I've accomplished
nothing this morning, I have white antelopes
words in my head, maybe a mantra
nothing lives long, only the earth and mountains

father's day

highwood cemetery
rush from morning sun
already too hot, I need shade
not looking at my feet
I stumble on the grave of my uncle

I hadn't remembered
he was buried here
for a second confused
I look at graves around
kusserow, a name lost
on the maternal side of my family

I never knew my uncle
he died ten years before
my arrival, kidney failure
barely twenty-one, it's no surprise
that no one really spoke of him
just as now, no one speaks of his other
brother gone, or his other brother gone

I only have some vague story
him placing garlic baloney
on the nose of a dog named seymour
making it sit still
before allowing the dog to flip
the treat, reap the reward

sometimes a day takes you
somewhere you didn't expect to go
it's father's day I figured
I should visit my father
who rests in the next cemetery over
whose grave takes some time to find

in the years after his death
my mother would come here
with her grief, sit on the grass
plant flowers and memories
as my brother and I
played around the stones
counted them, made stories up
while playing star wars or g.i joe

I've not been here often
a few times in the thirty years
since my mother remarried
I sit for a while
listen to hawks and jays
the traffic of marshall avenue
the blood in my veins
the roots of a tree of history
I came from the rush of this avenue

my sense of time, of place is acute
the way they bleed through memory
become tenuous, because time
and space do not measure
the way we conceive they do

d.a levy said
I have a city to cover with lines
I consider those lines
I trace those lines
> lines of family
> lines of history
> lines of a city

résumé

dear human resources manager
I know you get millions of pieces of paper
from job hungry applicants
that you don't give a fuck about
much as we don't give a fuck about you
but capitalism hasn't ended
I mean theoretically it ended
when the industrial revolution was pronounced dead
but capital's endless exploitation is still rampant
apparently just to live
                to experience life
is not an acceptable trade
I suppose it doesn't matter
that this is not meaningful work
there are mostly retail and service jobs
left for low-wage workers
who could only be so lucky
to dream of universal basic income
            or free health care
so I'll happily wait on americans
who believe that material possessions
will fill their empty hearts

I can't tell you what intangible qualities
I offer. I'm quick with new tasks
I've run businesses for friends dying of cancer
I work hard when there's work to be done

I think outside of the box
I write poems and daydream
I want to cry at least once a day
because the world is beautiful
because the world is sad
because I might be hungover
because existence is ultimately futile

I'll tell you I won't spend more than
two hours a day in the bathroom
writing poems
on paper, on the stall walls
if I choose the walls
I promise you'll have
the most articulate customers
I'll hide a dictionary
behind the toilet to help customers translate
since I have a penchant for five-dollar words
I'll volunteer my webster's
that I stole in eighth grade
it has space guns drawn in the margins
but it's served me well
for almost thirty years

I have no idea where I'll be in five years
in ten years, hell if any of us could see
that far into the future we wouldn't be
here looking for a fucking job
fuck if I'm even sure what I want to be
when I grow up, or maybe I know

but people don't pay poets money
people don't believe in art
people only believe
in money or a god that don't exist
they long for an afterlife
like I long for early retirement
I promise I won't say that out loud

it's safe to say I'm highly adaptable
last week I installed cabinets one day
hung a suspended ceiling the next
I sold records in my spare time
wrote and submitted poems
agreed to do another benefit show
then woke up and was a book mule
I drank beer on my break
because it tasted good
and I was tired
I learned a long time ago
you always say no in moderation

seriously, I've sold paint
been cursed at for not having the key
to the narcotics locker at a drug store I managed
I pretended to care about office supplies
sporting goods, deli meat, detailing cars
processing checks, auto parts
and I probably forgot a few

really, I'm happy to pretend to care
about whatever because I need a job
if however you drug test
I'm gonna test positive for marijuana
I know it's still sort of illegal
I promise I won't smoke it before
a shift or in the middle of a shift
generally, it's a sleep aid
and that's important for productivity

that's what you want
happy and productive workers
anesthetized and dreamless
wading through their lives
getting by
careening
at the drop edge of broke
a paycheck away from being hungry
a paycheck away from being homeless
a paycheck away from hope

the day job

(for nancy krieg)

we work till we're blind
figuratively perhaps
but when the garage door
goes up in the darkness
comes down in darkness
it becomes hard
to tell if we haven't
transformed into moles
then the days bleed together
and together and together
until they become a river
we can't actually see
for having our heads
under, the paycheck
gets no bigger, we stretch
and stretch and stretch
to the point of breaking
it's a wonder we even try to pretend
to be alright, all our heart
given out before we have time
to rest with ourselves
of course, the world seems crazy
of course, it feels insurmountable
we wait, look for a magic wand

something to clear cloud cover
a few minutes to feel human again
blank without the flow of the world
with the sun directly on our faces
breathlessly easy for a short while

elegy for the american dream

it's not when, it's if the car starts
it's when the bills come due
> you realize no matter how much
> you worked, it ain't enough

it's when you have to go to the doctor
> but you don't have insurance, even if you did
> there's deductibles

it's going to work so sick you can't stand, but you can't miss
> the pay

it's threatening yourself with the free clinic if you don't get
> better

it's choosing the gas bill or the electric bill this week
it's trying to stretch two meals from everything
it's standing in hours lines to drop off food stamp paperwork
> finally getting the interview to find you make $50
> more than the cutoff

it's peanut butter sandwiches, it's grilled cheese sandwiches
> every night
> you bought bread and you can't even let ends go to
> waste

it's shoplifting milk
it's making forty dollars last two weeks
it's counting quarters to buy gas
it's counting quarters to buy detergent
it's counting quarters till payday
it's chasing after you're pay
it's called cash strapped

it's the rent always being due
it's the collection agency on the phone at eight am
> everyday
> at least you don't need an alarm clock

it's realizing that minimum wage means you mean
> nothing

it's a ten-cent raise, or a quarter raise or a percentage
> that barely adds up to an extra $20 after taxes

it's having your debit card stolen and everything bounces
it's feeling rich when you get your tax return only to
> be broke the next day

it's always bottom shelf or in a box
it's not buying things new until the old is broken
it's trying to get by broken
it's regretting every transaction
it's counting wasted time
it's being too stressed to do anything
it's the two-job exhaustion
it's not saying no to cash side work or overtime
it's someone telling you to pull yourself up from you're
> bootstraps

it's the satisfaction of telling them *fuck off*

a cheeseburger on memorial day

I ordered a cheeseburger
and fries at the middle
eastern market cafeteria
cause its memorial day

memorial day
or decoration day
lip service holiday
for those that patriotically gave
the ultimate sacrifice

I enjoyed my cheeseburger
on memorial day, during ramadan
when muslims fast till sunset
I wanted to celebrate immigrants
the possibilities of a world without hate
a world where no one dies in wars
a world that doesn't exist
because of U.S foreign policy
because in the U.S we celebrate war

I thought as I finished my cheeseburger
on memorial day, of all the flags
planted like seeds in cemeteries that bloom in may
how it wouldn't take more than
a strong wind to blow all those flags away

on finding three hundred dollars in a book on FDR that I ordered off the internet

(for lori jakiela)

thank you
FDR
for paying
my rent
this month

a fedora and a mustache

in her mid-fifties
husband has cancer
in this untenable space
she calls to request *herbal* relief

she's nervous
can I say cookies
will alarm bells ring
will I be arrested immediately

she says
this was something you didn't do in my day
the fear of jail was too much

she asks
should I wear I a disguise
I could fedora
I could mustache
I could fake glasses

she changes the meeting
she texts the address
she says
look for the house
wearing a fedora
a mustache

kerouac go home

I hear the waitress' footfalls
they sound like roses as they echo
at avenue b, as they echo
at the avenue of the americas
at the intersection of bleecker
& mcdougal where silsbe can't
understand why there's so many people
sure, he's got a few drinks in him
but I never thought I'd see new yorkers
turn heads at open indictments of procreation
or at least procreation with the intent
to further the fading bulb of humanity

jay and ally say they used to write
kerouac go home on the men's room
wall at the white horse
dylan thomas bleeds out
the blood trail runs to the chelsea hotel
I slipped on it when I tried
to remember the last time I had a future

I tried to remember the last time
I saw the ocean, there were mustangs
racing on the garden state parkway
there were little hands waving on BQE
I swear there was a liberty torch
in the harbor, its head
struggling above the surface

I've snagged myself, a driftwood
sculpture, there is so much debris
the gulls have picked through
soft shelled and horseshoe crabs
the few untouched are boiling
to burst, but the ocean it still
waves under the twin eyes of lighthouses
it never bothered with magic or loss

wonder bread, chipped ham, tastycakes

it's not a real road
until you see a front-end loader
pulled over, horse collared
at the roadside by a cop car
right near the ass
of a wal-mart

I honestly forgot
it was memorial day
until I hit the hill
the cemetery stretching
festooned in hundreds
of flags, if there was a grave
to honor, you couldn't find
it in the wind

in town the football players
are walking to their cars
token flags and shoulder pads

this town was a stop
on the underground railroad
the supermarket has specials
on wonder bread, chipped ham
and tastycakes. the food truck
serves funnel cake and sno-cones

the veterans hang
from light posts, the bunting

in the windows, we only give
lip service to our wars, maybe no
one needs to know what a just war is
maybe we don't want to look that close

if we cared more maybe
the pizza shop on 4th wouldn't
have closed so long ago
that the weeds are up to the window

if we cared more we'd all
have two busted ass trans-ams
parked on our quarter acre manicured lawn
maybe if we cared more
we could afford one of those
ranch houses on utopia street

instead we run for the hills
this parade healed
in that same elemental way
as a sunday church service
we take away our lies
the misconceptions we swear
we're right about
hold them close
to our hearts
while we wait weeks
for the rain to wash
the piles of horse shit
that were left by the corner
of walnut street away

postcard from jeanette pennsylvania

there's a fight
outside the dollar general
somebody punched somebody
everybody was screaming
broken noses blossom

the party place
blares *happy birthday*
to an empty street

they sell bread
in the saint vincent depaul
day old or expired
for a quarter

everything here
costs a quarter
still, there's nothing
here I want

there are still
three italian restaurants
around town, the waitress
smells like christmas

I can't tell if she was born in 1952
or she died in 1952
but she's still here

maybe that's just how it is
when you watch
another version
and another version
and another version
of your life
crumble

beckemeyer illinois 1958

(for roy beckemeyer)

we usually headed to shoal creek
once I got older
it was carlyle lake
we'd find a dark alcove
toss our lines from shore
sometimes we'd use a boat
listen while the bow cut the water
my dad would tell us again
about how it was working in the mines
about everyone's brother or uncle gone
about the cave-ins, the explosions
about how they lost a hand, a leg
maybe if they're lucky only a finger
if they weren't maybe their lives
as I got older I took this as a reminder
to get out of town, to not let the mines
take me down and I listened

he would tell us again about our grandfather
a machine runner, how he was running
the air puncher when a ton of slate
came down on him, it shattered his back
they dug him out, took him to st. louis
it was too late, he was gone

no matter how many times he told the story
the hair on my neck stood up
the helmets we used on these nights
we're taken from the mines
I wondered then if the light
that shone above me
was the last light
my grandfather
had seen

new eagle pennsylvania 1960

he has a knack
for knowing
it's the hottest
day of the year

he comes home
from the mine
washes coal dust
from his face
his neck, his arms
changes into his
only pair of shorts

on his way
to the porch
he grabs
the beer
that's been
chilling for
over a year

he pops the top
sweat breaks
on his brow
coal dust mascara
runs down
his face

as long
as there's suds
in the bottle
he's completely free

a palomino and a bull snake

(for linzi garcia)

there were four water towers on the salina skyline
more than ten rooms with private baths where I stayed
I lived the last couple days on gin and tequila
there's been no need to hit the brakes over the last eighty miles
it feels like I'm barnstorming a prairie fire

the longest train I ever saw was in amarillo
that was before today, although it may have been sheridan
amarillo is four hundred miles south
sheridan is a palomino and a bull snake away

in the distance, there's a storm stuck over topeka
I've seen so much big sky, empty plains
It makes me wanna swing north for the badlands
I could make rapid city by morning

yesterday, I learned that mexican buffet
are the two most perfect words in the english language
as I left I noticed the only graffiti on the men's room wall
my asshole is burning
except the s's were faint, they'd been corralled
to some baptist ranch in the sky
where profanity is still the devil's tongue

yesterday, I learned how to turn breadcrumbs into bluebirds
if I head north, gun it to nebraska
I'm gonna try my luck turning motels into buffalo

beauty is a rare thing

on the back deck
of a civil war farmhouse
that survived gated in pimlico
you pulled out these perfectly
rolled joints, the reverend ran
into the woods to make water
on abandoned washer dryer combos

we watch the ghosts of owls
in an ancient walnut tree, you tell
me of your wife's affair, your daughter
and the relationship you struggle
to keep together. fritz the cat
sprays the basement floor
all your art piled up/ forgotten
age and time passing
depression its own hair trigger

I've heard it said
beauty is a rare thing
it seems my artist friends
know this and fear this equally
we scatter to document it
we post it where we can
proof this whole fucking human
experiment isn't completely
futile

that night we read in your shop
to six people, we ate in some
shitty bar in the inner harbor
you felt you had outlived yourself
depression pulled you in
I'm never sure you got back out

that night I couldn't sleep
I got lost in a painting
in the dining room
flipped through myriad
books of photography
thinking on all our
faulty human prayers

after a couple years
I saw you again
friends heard
you were struggling
we came to watch
baseball, talk records

I spent the evening djing
while friends raided every room
trying to get you to sell
impossibly rare lps

after all these years
working around music
I see it like paintings

like poems, like sculpture
as something you can't truly
own, we pass it, accept it
it feeds us as then we abandon
it to memory

I saw with each record
a look, painful
wash your face
you didn't understand
couldn't accept these things
were the sum of your legacy

after that depression
pulled you back I didn't
see you again, social media
tells me this mortal coil
finally shook you, I hope
somehow as you found
the end to this life
that life finally
gave you some peace

the ballad of dominic ierace

when my mother's second marriage
dissolved she spoke mostly in dreams
we were grown, still she wanted
to take us to disneyland
she wanted to buy a house
she wanted to keep us safe
after six years of rarely easy peace

she was forty something
working two jobs
circling the drain

I was barely twenty
working two jobs
circling the drain

neither of us could
afford a house alone
she asked me to cosign

after the jaggerz broke a massive
hit with *the rapper*
dominic ierace changed his name
had a few big hits regionally
with a band called the cruisers
if you live in pittsburgh
you hear *ah! leah* or
love is like a rock
regular as *stairway to heaven*

in the mid-nineties
ierace wrote mortgages
rock star life
confined to weekend warrior status

I recognized him
didn't care
never star struck
not by rock stars
not by mortgage brokers
he's professional, goofy
till my mom steps out

at the copy machine
his posture changes
he's relating to me
he wants to be remembered
as king cool, copier light glows
green, he shakes his head
it's a bitch, man

wishing rain on muskingum county

there's strange light
filtering through low
clouds. pinpricked they
burst with afternoon sun

central ohio
15 miles from zanesville
the pilot or love's or wilco
full of motion, light
in negative space going nowhere
wind shakes sycamore

a man comes from the bathroom
says it's more swamp here
as much piss on the floor
as anywhere else

I look up, affixed to light
I only want rain

postcard from blue ash

bleach white horizon
stark sun blinding
it seems from the highway
that ohio is the world
and the world is flat

past the last cloud
I could drop off the edge
of the world, find myself
on the bloomfield bridge
with night smelling of clove
cigarettes, stamped
out 20 years ago

I feel like ishmael
in this motel
where am I again?

blue ash, eyes peeled
bloodshot from the road
in this light my beard
is gun metal grey

I walk over to the door
pull it open to a night
of bad sleep and stars

it's 51 miles to vevay
indiana, a front
pushes the breeze
I breath deeply
I smell my lover
waiting

molotov party

there's a cold hap and harry's
between my legs
5 more hung on a ring
on the seat next to me

driving nashville's *safest* neighborhood
in the dark, big houses
sprawl gated, ghostly backlit
the ghost of andrew jackson's leg on display

it's nice the horse girls
and money men did well with
their hatchets, it's nice
the crime rate is low
money buys secrecy

cameras monitor beyond walls
I wait for police lights
sure no one who makes
under twenty k is allowed
in this neighborhood after dark

crickets so loud
you won't hear the fucking guillotine
so what would stop me
from buying every six-dollar bottle
of vodka from the package shop

with a stop at kroger for a box of rags
start my own molotov party

the proper arc or with good enough aim
I'll make six bills singe inconceivable million
dollar houses to ash

roadside piss, splash a wall
tag a camera with an empty
sirens crow in the distance
three beers down
flames off in the distance
belle meade plantation is burning

let it burn, let the minie balls
sing from the bodies of the dead
all the landmarks of those that owned
still feel you can own a human
should be smashed, burned
their history rewritten revealing
this class as parasites

we were to make democracy
every generation in our image
we failed, people are not free
the time is right to start again

spark the next cocktail
it has to start somewhere, who cares where it ends
tonight it burns, tomorrow it burns
the next revolution starts in nashville

these waters were dry

her grandparents were poor
the dirt farmer kind
at least her grandmother was
you could say her grandfather
was no account

everyday she'd find a bend
in the mississippi
net as many catfish as she could
fodder for an always growing brood

it may be exaggeration
they say she caught
fried so many
fucking catfish
these waters were dry
of them for several decades

her granddaughter catches catfish now
heads off, skin off
she leaves heads nailed
to the dock, to the fence
one more on the door
it's a vendetta

she leaves the heads hang
a reminder, a warning
not to trespass here again

legend has it
her grandmother was killed
by a catfish that walked like a man
it tarried across land, snuck in her house
one night, ate her grandmothers head

her granddaughter nails catfish heads
a warning, no catfish
will ever harm her family again

the confederate general of osage county

I breathe the breeze
from the wings of a fly
as sun cracks eyelids
hangover looks for a corner
and the same fucking rooster crows

this son of a bitch
the confederate general
of osage county, crows
every morning at the exact
time of stonewall jackson's
death, this son of a bitch
rooster believes in reincarnation

let us cross over the river
gather in the shade of the trees
let's roll out the trashcans
wait for the meth labs
of the gasconade to open
the ozarks will stand
then fall like appalachia
this son of a bitch keeps crowing

this rooster expects
lemons from your pocket
if you don't then motherfucker
you better at least straighten
up, stand at attention and salute

thunder alley

(for kell robertson and john dorsey)

wearing clean jeans
on the road is a luxury
today is all luxury

turkey vultures circle overhead
they smell the fox news
we picked up in a central
missouri bowling alley

dorsey and I
read kell robertson
in the driveway
under the osage sun

we are poets
out of place
noises in the dark
our disasters are voluntary

getting any feed for your chickens?
(for shawn pavey)

it's raining on kansas boulevard
city drains into warehouses
three tacos sit on the front seat
I find a parking lot, smother
them in spicy salsa
chase them with horchata
wait out the rain

eight hundred miles
through grasslands
riding on the ghost of buffalo
there's a diner with a green
chile cheeseburger waiting

this is closing in on some
twisted truckers hymn
six years on the road
I'm gonna eat well tonight
hey we can't all be dave dudley

shawn, you're right, we're shaved apes
poets shambling nowhere
crawling on our stomachs

there's been many nights
I've been within seconds
of jumping in my car

pedal down non-stop
until three days later
I find myself in the desert

usually in that moment
whoever I'm with realizes
I'm serious, starts to talk me down

you know brother, unemployment
warps one's mind, it should be
about finding yourself, instead
it's all pressure, inadequacy
redefining yourself by work
I've said it before
you are free, we all are
if you ever hear the phone ring
at six a.m. you find my voice
saying you got five hours
pack a bag, we're going
to albuquerque, you'll know
it's fucking serious, there's
cheeseburgers and chiles waiting
all we gotta do is get gone

breakfast in 1974

we were rambunctious
in the shadow of the first
world war, finding the midwest
smaller after the lights
the destruction of europe

maybe it was the depression
or our sons following
our footsteps years later
that took it out of us
maybe it was just living

now it's static
white noise daily
on the kansas horizon
waiting out our ends
in a 56 ford pickup
a.m. radio broken
on the same country station

we see each other
in the diners of morning
three eggs over easy
bacon coffee and toast
pile it in before the day

and its chores take over
saying the same things

another dusty western
wind saddled up
for breakfast in 1974

postcard from the flint hills

the earth was never flat
there are no dark spots
on the map with the inscription
there be monsters
I know this for certain
I've been spinning in circles
on a bluff in the flint hills
of kansas for all eternity
I've memorized every massive
sky, every shade of blue
I've named every cloud

when I close my eyes
hold my breath to fall though
the water of space
I know there is nothing
in the universe
that will ever catch me

the dust bowl again

railroad whistles whine
communist conductors
pray in train songs

these old wood houses
offer little shelter from wind
as the prairie howls, listen
you'll realize it's the ghost of the buffalo

this was the bottom
of the ocean
before it was
prairie, it will
never be prairie again

the desert waits
humans drink
the water table dry

the desert dreams
people are ghosts
this is the dust bowl again

postcard from ruidoso

the other side of this mountain
scorched by fire

burned out skeleton trees
offset by mazanita and sage

the frost of a full moon
headlights against the dark

ghost reflected
still on the withered bloom of yucca

kick at the sky

I crossed the rio bonito
barefoot, ice water
paralyzed in the sun

the current pushed
me to shore, cholla
still wearing blooms

there's a petroglyph here
reminder that
I did not cross alone

eight legs kick at the sky
furious, I step around
trail off for a mesquite stick

aid the tarantula
back to its understanding
of upright

there are no gifts in venom
I think it's well
past time we part ways

seventy-three miles from the state line

shimmer of windshields in the rearview
shimmer of windshields ahead
power lines reflect silver on a faded blue sky
turkey vultures, the smell of oil
cow and pronghorn constellations

my foot fell off the pedal miles ago
a still life
drifting forever
seventy-three miles from the state line

it was a golden time

been on the road
long enough now
to feel like three
mummified frogs
dried in a tejas mudpuddle

a woman in a wal-mart
parking lot shouts
I don't believe you
should leave a baby
in a car, even if it's running

I steal what I need
scoundrel hunter gatherer
from ancient time

there's a dead bear in an irrigation
ditch, it left me with the strange
feeling I've been here before

the windshield grows
a mustache, I see the world
clearer in my dreams
problem is I never
remember my dreams

climbing trees into arkansas

the smell of rain
comes strong
in dekalb

I spent today
climbing trees into arkansas
except where I started
there were no trees
only cotton and oil fields
badlands

there was an accident
on the highway behind me
cars and soldiers shot down in battle

there is nothing like rain
in arkansas, in little rock
south park street steps
between time machines

it shouldn't have to be this hard
to recognize everyone is human
that the occupants of this planet
are all one organism

it shouldn't be this hard
to hear the ghosts of history
until then this will never end

we are motels under construction
we are driving the wrong way
on the interstate

blind into leaving

I'm drinking beer
in a bourbon town again
the waitress raised eyebrows
suspicious, I lock eyes
on an alligator and a shark

the beltways of kentucky
are kind, no stress, no trucks
no cops. set the cruise
just north of 80, miles
dissolve easy, still
if I dive into bourbon
now, I'll be slobbering
in moments, there's some things
you can't drink away

guitar player works
statesboro blues
more allmann than mctell
the sunset was rosewater
in the rearview tonight
I wanted to hold my breath

waitress wants to know
if I need another
I need an I.V
she sees it, tells me
these are good people

it took three tries
to get a room
the lobby full bloom
appalachian floor show
every toilet full of shit

waitress brings me a third
I down it in one magic swallow
broke down engine
guzzles gasoline
wizard guitarist is on
fingerstyle sweet leaf
I tip, walk blind into leaving

from a motel 6

eyes focus through morning
I blink away miles
dreams

her hands turn to crows when she first wakes
she'd already be stirring coffee
in interrogation lights

she's not here
alone
inventory of places

where am I now?
where have I been?
how long has it been?
this trip exploded
into a million pieces

I explode
into a million pieces

these last miles
beg for mercy

where is home again?

Jason Baldinger was recently told he looks like a cross between a lumberjack and a genie. He's also been told he's not from Pittsburgh, but actually is the physical manifestation of Pittsburgh. Although he's unsure of either, he does love wandering the country writing poems. His newest books are *A Threadbare Universe* (Kung Fu Treachery Press), *The Afterlife is a Hangover* (Stubborn Mule Press) and *A History of Backroads Misplaced: Selected Poems 2010-2020* (Kung Fu Treachery). He also has a forthcoming book with James Benger called *This Still Life*. His work has been widely across print journals and online. You can hear him read his work on Bandcamp and on lp's by The Gotobeds and Theremonster.